THE KING &
His Bride

God's true purpose for marriage

David Mendoza III

www.booksforhisglory.com

THE KING & *His Bride*

God's true purpose for marriage

ISBN Hardcover: 979-8-9933809-5-7
ISBN Paperback: 979-8-9933809-4-0
ISBN eBook: 979-8-9933809-6-4

First Edition: February 2026

Printed in the United States of America

DEDICATION

To my beautiful Bride, I am so grateful for your unwavering support and your incredibly generous and loving spirit. Thank you for being my life partner and for standing by my side not just during the joyful moments, but also through the challenging times.

CONTENTS

chapter one

THE GODLY DESIGN OF MARRIAGE

The LORD God said, "It is not good for the man to be alone. I will make a helper suitable for him."

GENESIS 2:18

Marriage, once regarded as a sacred institution, has become increasingly unfamiliar in contemporary society. Its genuine significance and purpose have gradually faded, leaving behind a hollow echo of what it once represented. In the past, marriage was not merely a legal contract or social formality; it was a profound commitment—a union built on love, trust, and mutual respect. It symbolized the merging of two lives, families, and futures, grounded in shared values and aspirations.

Today, however, what we often observe is an imitation of that ideal. The essence of marriage has been diluted, as many who were meant to cherish and uphold its value have overlooked its true meaning. Rather than a partnership rooted in deep emotional connection and shared purpose, marriage has, for some, become a fleeting trend or status symbol—devoid of the commitment and dedication it once required.

Conversely, others enter marriage out of a desire for companionship or societal pressure without fully understanding its responsibilities and implications. Unrealistic expectations or a superficial understanding often lead to disillusionment and, ultimately, the dissolution of the union.

As a result, the sanctity of marriage is frequently compromised, with many viewing it as a temporary arrangement rather than a lifelong commitment. Rising divorce rates and the prevalence of cohabitation without marriage further illustrate this shift. The depth of connection marriage was intended to foster is often replaced by a transactional mindset, where personal fulfillment outweighs the shared journey of two individuals.

In this cultural landscape, the true value of marriage is overshadowed by shifting priorities and a lack of understanding of its foundational principles. This reality calls for a reevaluation of what marriage means today and a return to the core values that restore its purpose and significance. Only then can marriage be revived as a meaningful, cherished covenant rather than a mere formality or passing trend.

To understand how far society has strayed from the authentic purpose of marriage, we must examine its original design. Marriage is not a construct of human ingenuity, cultural influence, or religious tradition alone; it is a divine blueprint established by God—one that transcends time and human interpretation.

At its core, marriage is rooted in companionship and partnership. It is a sacred covenant that reflects a deeper spiritual truth, characterized by mutual love, respect, and support. Where two individuals come together to form a bond that is both intimate and enduring. This union serves not only the individuals involved but also fulfills a greater purpose within families, communities, and society.

Historically, marriage has provided stability and structure, forming the foundation of families where children are nurtured and values are passed from one generation to the next. Its original design emphasizes commitment and fidelity, creating a safe environment for growth and flourishing.

Yet in contemporary society, many of these principles

have been overshadowed or redefined. Individualism, shifting cultural values, and evolving social norms have redirected the focus from collective good and covenantal commitment to self-fulfillment and personal expression. Technology and social media further complicate relationships, often fostering superficial connections that undermine the depth and perseverance marriage requires.

To grasp the extent of this deviation, we must return to the divine blueprint. This involves embracing love, sacrifice, service, and a shared commitment to grow together through life's challenges. Marriage is not merely a contract or social arrangement; it is a sacred covenant that demands dedication and endurance.

During the time of the prophet Jeremiah, God's people strayed from their covenant, abandoning righteous principles in favor of false idols. Though God pleaded with them in Jeremiah 6:16 to return to the ancient paths, they refused. This pattern mirrors many modern marriages—including those within the church—that have drifted from God's intended path.

When we lose our way, wisdom calls us to pause and retrace our steps rather than wander aimlessly. To restore our marriages, God urges us to return to His original design— the ancient path. It is time to embrace it once again.

The Original Design

In Genesis chapter two, we encounter a pivotal moment in the creation story. God observes Adam, the first human, living in the beauty and abundance of the Garden of Eden—yet alone. Nothing in the environment is lacking, yet something essential is missing. Adam's solitude reveals a deeper emotional and relational need that creation itself cannot fulfill.

As Adam names the animals, he begins to notice a pattern. Each creature has a counterpart, a partner with whom life is shared. These pairings reflect companionship woven into the very fabric of creation. In contrast, Adam stands alone, without someone to walk alongside him, share responsibility, or truly understand his experience. God's response is striking: "It is not good for the man to be alone." This statement highlights a truth that remains deeply relevant today—human beings are designed for meaningful connection.

God responds to this need by creating a suitable helper for Adam, establishing the foundation for partnership. This was not a solution to boredom or convenience, but a deliberate design for shared life. From the beginning, marriage was meant to be a cooperative relationship in which two people work together, support one another, and carry life's responsibilities side by side.

The word *helper* often carries negative connotations in modern culture, suggesting inferiority, passivity, or a secondary role. However, the original Hebrew word used in Genesis—*ezer*—communicates something far different. *Ezer* speaks of strength, assistance, and essential support, not subordination.

Throughout Scripture, *ezer* is frequently used to describe God Himself as a helper to His people. This usage alone reshapes how we should understand the term. God's help is not weak or secondary; it is powerful, sustaining, and often the difference between defeat and survival. In military contexts, *ezer* refers to reinforcements—those who arrive with strength when it is most needed. A helper, then, is not someone who stands behind, but someone who comes alongside.

Applied to marriage, *ezer* describes a partnership built on mutual dependence rather than hierarchy. It acknowledges that both individuals bring strengths, insights, and perspectives the other does not possess alone. Marriage was never intended to be a relationship where one person carries the emotional, spiritual, or practical weight by themselves. Instead, it is a shared journey where each partner plays a vital role.

Many couples experience strain when one person feels unseen, unheard, or unsupported. Over time, this imbalance can create resentment, emotional distance, and eventually a breakdown of the relationship. Understanding marriage through the lens of *ezer* challenges couples to ask important questions: *Do we support one another when life becomes heavy? Do we listen with empathy? Do we value our partner's contributions, even when they differ from our own?*

When couples embrace this original design, marriage becomes less about competition or control and more about cooperation. It fosters respect, collaboration, and shared purpose. Each partner is valued not for what they provide alone, but for how they strengthen the relationship together. In this kind of partnership, both individuals are empowered to grow, and the marriage itself becomes a place of safety, resilience, and connection.

This understanding of marriage—rooted in partnership rather than power—offers hope to couples struggling with disconnection or contemplating divorce. When both people commit to being a source of strength and support for one another, marriage can move from survival to renewal, and from isolation to shared life.

The Garden

Marriage is a divine blessing meant to enrich human life, representing a profound bond between two people and, for believers, between humanity and the Creator. It is more than a social contract or legal agreement; marriage is a covenant—a committed relationship built on trust, devotion, and shared responsibility.

At its best, marriage reflects love that is intentional, enduring, and life-giving. When grounded in faith, it becomes a visible expression of grace, mercy, and unconditional love. Even for those who do not identify as people of faith, marriage at its healthiest offers stability, meaning, and connection that extend beyond the couple themselves.

From the beginning, God's vision for humanity was one of goodness, beauty, and harmony. Rather than placing human beings in chaos or isolation, He placed them in a garden—a space of peace, provision, and relationship. The Garden of Eden was not merely a physical setting; it symbolized the kind of life God intended for humanity: one marked by connection, safety, purpose, and intimacy. Within this environment, relationship was central—not only between humanity and God, but between man and woman as well.

The creation of both man and woman in God's likeness

reveals that partnership was not an afterthought but a deliberate design. Marriage was established as a relationship in which two people could grow together, support one another, and share life's responsibilities.

This partnership was meant to reflect unity without erasing individuality—two distinct people walking together in shared purpose. In this sense, marriage mirrors balance: closeness without control, unity without loss of identity.

The intention behind marriage is not rooted in obligation but in love. It is an invitation to experience life more fully—through shared joy, mutual support, and perseverance through difficulty.

In a culture that often emphasizes independence, self-interest, and personal fulfillment above all else, marriage offers a different vision. It calls people to consider another's needs alongside their own, to practice patience, forgiveness, and commitment, and to build something lasting together.

For Christian couples, a Christ-centered marriage reflects God's redemptive love—modeled after Christ's selfless love for the Church.

This kind of love is not dependent on emotions or circumstances but is anchored in commitment. It seeks to encourage, uplift, and remain faithful even when relationships are strained or imperfect. For non-Christian couples, these same principles—selflessness, loyalty, grace, and perseverance—are equally essential for a strong and enduring marriage.

The impact of a healthy marriage reaches far beyond the couple. Families are shaped by the quality of the marital relationship, and the values practiced within the home influence future generations. Children who grow up witnessing love, respect, and commitment are more likely to carry those values into their own relationships.

In this way, marriage becomes a stabilizing force not only for individuals, but for families and communities as well.

Ultimately, marriage is meant to be a place of growth, safety, and shared purpose—a modern reflection of the garden where it all began.

When couples commit to nurturing their relationship with intention and care, marriage can become a space where both individuals are strengthened and where hope, healing, and connection can flourish.

It is a covenant that reflects the heart of God himself—one that invites two people to walk together, build together, and grow together over time.

A Counterfeit

The enemy's agenda has remained unchanged since the beginning of time: to kill, steal, and destroy (John 10:10). This mission flows from a deep hatred for anything that originates from God. Marriage, designed by God and reflective of His covenantal love, is therefore a prime target. The enemy's goal is not merely to disrupt individual lives but to undermine what God has declared good, holy, and life-giving.

When the enemy encounters a marriage united in faith, love, and purpose, it stands as a living testimony to God's design. Such a union reflects the relationship between Christ and His Church—a relationship marked by commitment, sacrifice, and enduring love. This reality is something the enemy can never replicate. Unable to create, he seeks instead to corrupt, distort, and dismantle. What he cannot possess, he attempts to destroy.

The enemy operates strategically, often subtly. His tactics are rarely obvious or dramatic; more often, they are quiet, persuasive, and emotionally convincing. He exploits exhaustion, disappointment, unmet expectations, and unresolved conflict. He understands that if he can weaken a couple's relationship with God, he can more easily weaken their relationship with one another.

One of his most effective strategies is the use of counterfeits—offering substitutes for what God has already provided. These counterfeits promise fulfillment, relief, or happiness but deliver emptiness and regret. They distort reality, making couples believe that joy, peace, or intimacy can be found outside of God's design rather than restored within it. For married couples, this often begins with subtle thoughts: *You shouldn't have to work this hard. Your spouse doesn't understand you. You deserve to be happy.* While these thoughts may feel reasonable, they can slowly shift the heart away from covenant and toward self-protection or escape. Over time, gratitude is replaced by comparison, and commitment is replaced by contemplation of alternatives.

The enemy frequently magnifies a spouse's flaws while minimizing their strengths. He encourages spouses to replay offenses while forgetting moments of faithfulness. He whispers that distance is permanent, that change is impossible, and that the marriage is beyond repair. In doing so, he shifts the focus from what God can restore to what feels broken beyond hope.

In some cases, he introduces the idea of another relationship—someone who seems more attentive, more affirming, or more understanding. This illusion can feel like relief, but it is ultimately destructive. What appears to be an answer to pain often becomes a deeper wound. The enemy never reveals the full cost of his counterfeits until the damage is done.

His lies are consistent and persuasive: *What you don't have is better than what you do have.* This deception fuels discontent and creates a perpetual sense of lack. Couples caught in this cycle may find themselves constantly striving for something more, while overlooking the blessings, history, and potential growth within their marriage.

For Christian couples, discernment is essential. Not every thought is truth, and not every feeling should be followed. Scripture reminds us to take our thoughts captive and to measure them against God's Word. When we begin to view our marriage through the lens of frustration rather than faith, we become vulnerable to deception.

The battle for marriage is ultimately spiritual, but its effects are deeply practical. Remaining vigilant means choosing forgiveness when resentment feels easier, choosing communication over silence, and choosing prayer over isolation. It means inviting God into the tension rather than assuming He has abandoned the struggle.

By anchoring ourselves in God's truth and staying connected to Him, couples can recognize the enemy's schemes and refuse his counterfeits. Restoration begins when spouses turn toward God and toward one another, trusting that what He designed, He is also able to heal. In doing so, marriage becomes not only protected, but strengthened—standing as a testimony of God's faithfulness in a world desperate for hope.

The Fall

In Genesis 3, the narrative unfolds with the adversary approaching Eve in the form of a serpent. This moment invites us to consider two important questions: Why did he choose to appear as a serpent, and why did he approach Eve rather than Adam? Both questions offer insight into the nature of temptation and its impact on relationships—particularly marriage.

The serpent was not a random choice. One of the enemy's most effective strategies is to approach us through what feels familiar and non-threatening. Temptation rarely arrives in obvious or alarming forms; instead, it often comes through what we already know, trust, or feel comfortable with. As James 1:14 explains, we are drawn away by our own desires. The enemy exploits existing vulnerabilities rather than introducing something entirely new.

The serpent was a recognized part of Eve's environment. Its familiarity lowered her defenses and created a false sense of safety. When we feel at ease, we are more likely to let our guard down. In the same way, temptation often enters our lives—and our marriages—through familiar voices, trusted relationships, or seemingly harmless thoughts. What feels safe can quietly become dangerous when discernment is absent.

By appearing as a creature already present in the garden, the enemy bypassed Eve's natural caution. This strategic use of comfort allowed him to plant seeds of doubt without resistance. Temptation is most effective when it feels reasonable, justified, or even harmless.

The serpent's approach also reveals the threefold nature of temptation. He appealed to the desires of the flesh, the allure of the eyes, and the temptation of pride. By suggesting that the fruit was good for food, he appealed to physical desire. By emphasizing that it was pleasing to the eye, he engaged Eve's senses. By promising wisdom and likeness to God, he targeted pride—the desire to elevate oneself beyond God's design.

These same patterns often appear in marital struggles.

Physical desires, emotional longings, and wounded pride can distort judgment. When unmet needs or unresolved hurts are left unaddressed, temptation can feel like an answer rather than a threat. What seems appealing in the moment may ultimately lead to deeper brokenness.

The temptation of pride is particularly destructive. The serpent suggested that Eve could gain wisdom and autonomy apart from God. Pride convinces us that we know better, that our feelings justify our actions, or that obedience is optional when it feels inconvenient. In marriage, pride can manifest as defensiveness, refusal to take responsibility, or the belief that one's needs outweigh the covenant itself.

The serpent's decision to approach Eve rather than Adam also reveals the enemy's strategic thinking. According to 1 Timothy 2:14, Eve was deceived, while Adam sinned knowingly. Adam had received God's command directly, making him a more difficult target. The enemy instead sought to influence Adam indirectly by deceiving Eve, exploiting the relational bond between them.

This pattern continues today. When one spouse becomes discouraged, deceived, or emotionally isolated, the marriage becomes vulnerable. The enemy often works through division—miscommunication, silence, or misplaced trust—

rather than open confrontation. When spouses stop standing together in truth, they become easier to separate.

Eve's interaction with the serpent involved questioning God's word. Doubt was introduced before disobedience occurred. Once God's truth was distorted, deception followed naturally. This moment disrupted the intended order of trust and obedience, leading both Adam and Eve into sin.

Adam's response is equally significant. He was not deceived; he made a conscious choice to disobey. His decision illustrates the weight of responsibility and the power of free will. Adam chose relationship over obedience—but without leadership or truth. This decision fractured humanity's relationship with God and altered the course of history.

The consequences were immediate. Shame replaced innocence. Fear replaced intimacy. Blame replaced unity. What was once harmonious became fractured. These effects are still visible in marriages today. When trust is broken or truth is compromised, distance quickly follows.

The story of the Fall reminds us that our choices never affect us alone. Decisions made in moments of weakness can ripple through our marriages, families, and generations. In marriage, unaddressed sin, unresolved conflict, or unchecked temptation can quietly erode trust and intimacy over time.

In a culture that often prioritizes individual desires over shared responsibility, this narrative calls couples back to awareness and unity. Marriage requires vigilance, humility, and mutual accountability. When spouses recognize their interconnectedness and choose faithfulness—even when it is difficult—they resist division and create space for healing.

The Fall marks the beginning of brokenness, but it also points to the need for redemption. As this chapter closes, it prepares the way for hope—the hope that what was broken can be restored, and what was lost can be redeemed. God's design for marriage did not end in the garden, and neither does His desire to heal and renew what has fallen.

Chapter One Reflection

Marriage is a sacred gift from God, designed for partnership, growth, and shared purpose. As we reflect on God's intention, we are reminded that marriage is more than a relationship—it is a covenant, a reflection of His love and faithfulness.

Sometimes, in the busyness of life, we forget that our marriages are meant to be places of mutual support, understanding, and spiritual growth. The challenges, temptations, and brokenness we encounter are not signs of God abandoning us, but reminders of our need to return to Him and lean on His wisdom.

True restoration in marriage begins with hearts aligned to God's will. When we cultivate humility, love, and a willingness to follow His guidance, we create space for healing, grace, and lasting unity. Even in seasons of struggle, God's presence can transform pain into purpose, weakness into strength, and division into deepened connection.

Chapter One Prayer

Heavenly Father,

Thank You for the gift of marriage, forgive us for the times we have strayed from Your path or allowed pride, selfishness, or distraction to interfere in our relationships. Teach us to honor You in our marriages, to love with patience and grace, and to support one another as You intended.

Strengthen our hearts to resist the enemy's deception and to embrace Your wisdom. May our marriages reflect Your love, bring glory to Your name, and serve as a witness of Your faithfulness in a world that so desperately needs hope.

In Jesus' name, Amen.

Practical Takeaway

- *Center Your Marriage on God Daily* – Take intentional moments each day to pray together or individually, asking God to guide your thoughts, words, and actions in the relationship. Even five minutes of focused prayer or reflection can create a spiritual anchor.

- *Practice Active Support* – Look for ways to come alongside your spouse as a true helper ("ezer"), offering encouragement, listening without judgment, and valuing their strengths. Small gestures of support build trust and reinforce your partnership.

- *Identify and Resist Temptation Early* – Be mindful of influences or thoughts that lead you away from unity—whether pride, distraction, or comparison. Pause, pray, and ask God to redirect your heart toward forgiveness, patience, and His design for your marriage.

- *Return to the "Ancient Path"* – When conflict or distance arises, step back and ask: "Am I following God's plan for our marriage, or my own desires?" Let Scripture guide your decisions and prioritize restoration over defensiveness.

chapter two

A DIVINE UNION

"Therefore what God has joined together, let no one separate."

MARK 10:9

God formed them male and female, for this reason a man will leave his father and mother and united to his wife. The two will become one flesh, so they are no longer two, but one flesh (Mark 10:6-8). This divine design is not merely a biological or social construct; it embodies a deeper spiritual truth that recognizes the unique roles and contributions of both genders in the tapestry of life. This union shows a deep understanding of how human relationships work together. It highlights the important balance and connection between the two.

Moreover, this collaboration underscores the importance of adaptability and compromise, as both parties navigate challenges and celebrate successes together. It serves as a reminder that the strength of a relationship lies not only in the moments of agreement but also in the ability to work through differences and find common ground.

My wife and I often find it challenging to agree on things, but when we finally reach a compromise, the results are usually much better than I expected. It's a journey that requires patience, understanding, and a willingness to see things from each other's perspectives. During the process of building our home, we had to meet with the designer from time to time, and let me tell you, he could have easily been a marriage counselor with the way we debated our preferences. He was incredibly patient, guiding us through the myriad of choices while skillfully navigating our differing opinions.

There were moments of tension, of course, as we both had our visions of what our dream home should look like. I remember one particularly heated discussion about the kitchen layout—my wife envisioned an open space that flowed seamlessly into the living area, while I was adamant about having a more traditional, compartmentalized design. It took several meetings, countless sketches, and a lot of back-and-forth before we finally found a middle ground that satisfied us both.

Now, as I look around our home, I can't help but smile and feel grateful for its beauty. Each room tells a story of our collaboration, our willingness to listen, and our ability to compromise. Our home truly represents our love, commitment, and the journey we took together to create a space that feels uniquely ours. From the brick color that we painstakingly selected to the elegant arches that frame our entryway, and the carefully chosen light fixtures that cast a warm glow in the evenings, every detail reflects our shared affection and the countless hours we spent discussing, debating, and ultimately deciding together.

It's more than just a house; it's a testament to our partnership. The living room, with its cozy seating arrangement, is where we gather to unwind after a long day, and the kitchen, now a harmonious blend of both our ideas, is where we create meals and memories together. Each corner of our home is infused with the essence of our relationship, reminding us that while we may not always see eye to eye, the compromises we make can lead to something truly beautiful. In the end, our home stands as a symbol of our love story, a place where we can continue to grow together, cherishing the journey that brought us here.

Ultimately, this partnership exemplifies the profound impact that strong, balanced relationships can have on personal and professional growth, illustrating how the synergy created by two individuals can lead to greater achievements than either could accomplish alone. It is a testament to the power of connection and the transformative potential that arises when a couple comes together with a shared purpose and commitment to one another.

Disagreements are an inevitable part of the human experience; they are woven into the very fabric of our interactions. Each individual carries a unique set of beliefs, values, and perspectives shaped by their personal experiences, upbringing, and environment. This diversity of thought is not limited to our romantic partners; in fact, we often find ourselves in conflict with a variety of people throughout our daily lives. Whether it's a colleague at work who has a different approach to a project, a friend who disagrees with our opinion on a movie, or even a family member with contrasting views on a holiday tradition, disagreements are a common thread that connects us all.

However, the intensity of disagreements can feel magnified in our relationships with our spouses. This heightened emotional response can be attributed to the sheer amount of time we spend together over the years. Living in close proximity means that we are more likely to encounter each other's quirks, habits, and differing opinions on a daily basis. The intimacy of a marital relationship often leads to deeper emotional investments, making conflicts feel more personal and significant. When we are in a committed partnership, the stakes can feel higher, and the potential for hurt can be greater, which can lead to more intense disagreements.

In the context of marriage, the Bible offers wisdom in Song of Solomon 2:15, which advises couples to address minor issues before they escalate into larger conflicts: "Catch for us the foxes, the little foxes that ruin the vineyards, our vineyards that are in bloom." This metaphor highlights the importance of recognizing and dealing with small problems before they grow into something more damaging. In many marriages, it is not the major conflicts that create the most trouble; rather, it is the accumulation of smaller, seemingly insignificant issues that can gradually build up and snowball into significant problems.

These "little foxes" can take many forms—misunderstandings, unspoken grievances, or even minor annoyances that, if left unaddressed, can lead to resentment and larger disputes. By proactively communicating and resolving these smaller issues, couples can maintain a healthier relationship and prevent the deterioration of their emotional connection. It is essential for partners to cultivate an environment where open dialogue is encouraged, allowing them to express their feelings and concerns without fear of judgment or escalation.

Ultimately, while disagreements are a natural part of any relationship, how we handle them can make all the difference. By acknowledging the inevitability of conflict and committing to addressing the smaller issues before they grow, couples can strengthen their bond and foster a more harmonious partnership.

Catching the Little Foxes: Practical Steps for Couples

Small issues can quietly grow into major conflicts if left unaddressed. Here are some practical ways to identify and resolve the "little foxes" before they harm your marriage:

Schedule Regular Check-Ins - Set aside time each week to talk about your relationship—your highs, your lows, and any small frustrations that may have arisen. These conversations don't need to be formal or long; even 20–30 minutes of honest dialogue can prevent misunderstandings from building up.

Tip: Start by asking, "Is there anything small that's bothering you this week?" Encourage honesty without judgment.

Practice Active Listening - When your spouse shares a concern, focus on truly hearing them without interrupting or immediately defending yourself. Reflect back what they said to confirm understanding.

Example:

- Spouse: "I felt overlooked when you didn't ask about my day."
- Response: "I hear that you felt overlooked when I didn't check in. I understand that made you feel unappreciated."

This shows validation and prevents small frustrations from escalating.

Address Issues Promptly - Don't wait for "the perfect time" to bring up minor irritations. The longer small issues sit, the more likely resentment will grow. Approach the conversation with humility and love, focusing on your feelings rather than placing blame.

Tip: Use "I" statements instead of "You" statements. For example, "I feel stressed when…" instead of "You always…"

Identify Patterns, Not Isolated Incidents - Some disagreements are repetitive. Pay attention to recurring issues and discuss the root cause rather than just the symptom. Understanding the underlying needs—whether emotional, practical, or spiritual—can turn conflict into a growth opportunity.

Celebrate Small Wins - When a disagreement is resolved or a compromise is reached, acknowledge it. Celebrate the effort and progress, not just the outcome. This reinforces positive behavior and encourages collaboration in future challenges.

Example: Share a small gesture of appreciation: "I really appreciate how we worked through that kitchen layout together. It means a lot that we found a compromise."

Pray Together - For Christian couples, prayer is a powerful tool to align hearts and minds. Invite God into the conversation and ask for wisdom, patience, and unity. Praying together helps couples focus on shared values rather than individual ego, reminding both partners that they are on the same team.

Seek Outside Support When Needed - Sometimes, the little foxes persist despite your best efforts. Seeking counsel from a trusted mentor, pastor, or Christian counselor can provide guidance and practical tools for handling recurring challenges. There is no shame in asking for help—it's a sign of commitment, not weakness.

By intentionally addressing small issues before they grow, couples can create a home filled with respect, love, and harmony. Each conversation, compromise, and act of understanding strengthens the bond and ensures that minor irritations never undermine the greater joy and purpose of the marriage.

Marriage is a daily practice, not a one-time event. Catching the little foxes equips couples to navigate life's challenges together, deepening intimacy and fostering a lasting partnership that reflects God's design and grace.

A Divided Mindset

We don't have specific details about how long Adam and Eve spent in the Garden of Eden, but we do know that during their time there, Adam enjoyed a close, intimate relationship with God. Genesis 3:8 tells us that God walked in the garden in the cool of the day, seeking fellowship with humanity. This image highlights God's original design for humanity: to live in communion with Him, experiencing His presence, guidance, and love in a perfect environment.

The fact that both man and woman were created in God's image is profoundly significant. They were designed to reflect God's character and attributes—love, creativity, wisdom, and rationality. This divine image implies that they existed in holiness, untainted by sin, and filled with the Spirit of God. Their lives in the Garden were marked by purity, harmony, and a clear understanding of their purpose.

Recognizing that men and women are inherently different is crucial for understanding relationship dynamics. These differences are not flaws; they are blessings. Each gender brings unique strengths, perspectives, and abilities to the table. When embraced, these distinctions can enrich communication, decision-making, and emotional connection. For example, men and women often approach problem-solving and conflict differently: one may prioritize logic while the other prioritizes empathy. When these approaches are combined in mutual respect, solutions are more comprehensive, and relationships deepen.

The complementary nature of male and female traits fosters unity and partnership. In marriage and family, these differences create a balanced environment where both partners can thrive. When each individual values the other's strengths, they build a foundation of support and cooperation. Recognizing that these traits were divinely designed encourages couples to celebrate differences rather than perceive them as threats.

In the Garden, Adam and Eve exemplified how humanity was intended to interact with God and one another. Their creation in God's image underscores the importance of appreciating gender differences as a gift—one that enhances life and relationships rather than diminishes them. Embracing these differences can lead to richer, more fulfilling marriages, fostering love, respect, and purpose.

God intentionally imbued man and woman with distinct qualities meant to work in harmony. Traditionally, the man was seen as embodying strength, responsibility, and rational thought, while the woman exemplified nurturing, intuition, and emotional insight. Together, these traits created a balanced partnership designed to uplift, support, and complement each other. When both partners contributed their God-given strengths, the relationship functioned as a harmonious reflection of divine design.

However, the fall of humanity introduced a profound shift. Sin disrupted this harmony, and the complementary differences that once united man and woman became sources of conflict. Traits meant to strengthen the partnership were now often perceived as challenges or threats to one's own identity and desires. Misunderstanding and miscommunication replaced mutual support, creating tension and division.

This disruption extended beyond personal relationships, influencing societal norms and cultural expectations. Gender roles became rigid, often suppressing the full potential of both men and women. Where collaboration and unity were intended, competition and misunderstanding took root, perpetuating cycles of conflict and resentment.

For couples today, this history offers both insight and hope. Understanding that these conflicts are not merely personal failures but symptoms of a deeper spiritual reality can shift perspective. Marriage is meant to be a partnership that honors differences, not a battlefield where individual desires dominate. By embracing each other's God-given qualities, couples can transform conflict into collaboration.

A Solid Foundation

Divorce deeply grieves the heart of God. In *Malachi 2:16*, Scripture tells us that God hates divorce—not because He lacks compassion for those who experience it, but because He understands the profound damage it causes. Marriage was never meant to be a temporary agreement or a legal arrangement of convenience; it was designed as a sacred covenant, a living reflection of the relationship between God and His people.

In Hebrew, the word commonly associated with divorce comes from *karath*, meaning "to cut off" or "to sever." This word choice is intentional and sobering. Divorce is not simply the ending of a relationship; it is the tearing apart of something God intended to be woven together for life. It is the breaking of a union where two lives, hearts, and purposes were meant to function as one.

The impact of divorce reaches far beyond the couple involved. Its effects ripple outward, touching children, extended family members, friendships, and entire communities. Children often carry the heaviest burden, experiencing confusion, grief, insecurity, and loss. The stability they once knew can be shaken, leaving emotional wounds that may influence their future relationships and sense of trust.

Families, too, feel the fracture. Roles shift, loyalties feel divided, and relationships that once felt safe can become strained. Friends and loved ones may feel caught in the middle, unsure how to support both sides without taking part in the pain. Even within the broader community, divorce can alter social dynamics and support systems, reminding us that no marriage exists in isolation.

There is no such thing as an "easy" divorce. Even when separation seems necessary, the emotional consequences often linger long after legal matters are resolved. Pain, regret, grief, and fear can shape how individuals view love, commitment, and vulnerability in the future. Healing is possible, but it often requires time, intentional effort, and deep grace.

The reason God hates divorce is not rooted in condemnation but in love. He sees the beauty of marriage as a reflection of Christ and His Bride—the Church. God knows that marriage is a holy unity, where two souls are intricately joined into one. What He hates is the destruction of something so sacred and life-giving.

While Scripture is clear that God hates divorce, it is equally clear that **God never condones abuse**—emotional, physical, sexual, or spiritual. Remaining in an abusive relationship is *not* an act of faith, obedience, or endurance. Abuse is a violation of God's design for marriage and a distortion of covenant love.

It must be stated plainly: **It is never God's will for anyone to remain in an abusive relationship.** Seeking safety is not a lack of faith—it is an act of wisdom and courage. God's heart is for restoration, but restoration cannot exist where there is ongoing harm and unrepentant violence.

A solid foundation in marriage is built on love, safety, respect, and mutual submission under Christ—not fear or control. Where abuse exists, God's grace calls for protection, truth, and healing, not endurance of injustice.

Jesus reinforces the importance of foundation in *Matthew 7:24–27*, where He compares life to building a house. The wise person builds on the rock, while the foolish person builds on sand. When storms come—and they always do—the house built on the rock stands firm, while the one built on sand collapses.

Marriage is no different. Storms will come: conflict, disappointment, hardship, and seasons of doubt. The question is not whether challenges will arise, but what the marriage is built upon. When a marriage is grounded in God's Word and anchored in Christ, it has the strength to endure pressure without falling apart.

Many marriages begin with good intentions but are unknowingly built on unstable foundations. Often, we enter marriage driven by personal desires—hoping our spouse will meet unmet needs, heal old wounds, or fill spiritual emptiness. When Christ is absent from the center of our lives, we can unintentionally place expectations on our spouse that no human being can fulfill.

This can lead to disappointment and resentment, as marriage becomes a pursuit of self-fulfillment rather than a partnership rooted in mutual love, sacrifice, and shared faith. No spouse was ever meant to replace God in our lives.

Another major challenge to building a solid foundation is the emotional baggage we bring into marriage. Unresolved wounds from childhood, past relationships, abandonment, or betrayal often shape how we think, react, and communicate. Without healing, these experiences can distort expectations and create defensive patterns that hinder intimacy and trust.

These unaddressed wounds can affect how we interpret conflict, respond to criticism, or express affection. They can quietly sabotage communication and prevent couples from fully experiencing the joy and unity God intended for marriage.

True restoration begins when couples choose to start fresh—not by ignoring the past, but by placing Christ at the center of their relationship. When our primary love is rooted in Him, it naturally overflows into *agapē* love for one another— love that is patient, selfless, and unconditional.

Building a marriage on Christ allows the foundation to be shaped by grace rather than fear, by truth rather than past pain. Instead of reacting from wounds, couples learn to respond from love. Instead of striving to protect themselves, they learn to serve one another.

A solid foundation does not eliminate challenges, but it provides stability when they arise. When Christ is the cornerstone, marriage becomes a place of healing, growth, and restoration—a living testimony of God's redemptive design. Marriage built on the Rock can withstand the storms. And even when cracks appear, God's grace remains strong enough to rebuild what seems broken.

What Are You Building?

When constructing a home—or any structure—having a blueprint is essential. Without one, the builder is left guessing, often resulting in confusion, wasted effort, and instability. In the same way, many couples enter marriage with sincere hopes for growth and fulfillment, yet attempt to navigate it without spiritual direction. Without a clear foundation or guiding truth, even the best intentions can lead to frustration and collapse.

I understand this deeply. I married my wife at a young age, and at the time, we were both just starting out in life. We had enthusiasm, passion, and a strong desire to be together— but very little understanding of what marriage truly required. Looking back, we were excited, hopeful, and completely unprepared.

Like many young couples, we believed love alone would be enough. As teenagers, we thought we had life figured out. We lacked strong role models and had no real spiritual guidance. The only thing we felt confident about was our love for each other and our belief that we would be together forever.

Both of us grew up in broken families. Our parents had also married young, and while they loved us, their experiences unintentionally taught us more about what *not* to do than how to build a healthy marriage. We observed the consequences of unresolved conflict, unmet expectations, and emotional wounds. Yet, despite seeing those pitfalls, we still found ourselves repeating many of the same patterns.

At the beginning, both our parents—and later, we ourselves—entered marriage without a clear strategy, simply hoping for the best. But hope without direction rarely leads to the desired destination. How can anyone arrive where they want to go if they don't know which path to take?

For many years, my wife and I dreamed of a strong, fulfilling marriage—one marked by love, understanding, and companionship. But the reality we lived was far from that vision. Despite our efforts, it often felt like the harder we tried, the further away we drifted from the marriage we wanted. Instead of growing closer, we grew frustrated, disconnected, and weary.

A major reason for this was the emotional baggage we both carried into the marriage. Our foundation was already cracked. We tried to build something meaningful on unstable ground, and inevitably, everything we constructed began to crumble.

In our attempt to fill the emptiness we felt, we turned to unhealthy substitutes. Alcohol, superficial relationships, and career pursuits became distractions from the deeper issues we were unwilling—or unable—to face. Without realizing it, we were hurting one another while trying to survive. We wanted to love well, but we didn't know how. We were attempting to give what we ourselves did not possess.

After ten years of marriage, we were barely holding on. Eventually, everything unraveled. The love and effort we had poured into the relationship felt buried under layers of pain, disappointment, and regret. It seemed as though nothing was improving—only deteriorating.

One morning, on my way to work, I felt an overwhelming urge to pull over to the side of the road. In that moment, I knew I had reached my breaking point. Deep down, I knew the answer to my struggle—or rather, I knew *who* the answer was. Yet I had spent years running from Him, avoiding the very source of peace and direction I desperately needed.

God had been pursuing me all along, but I believed I could do life better on my own. At eleven years old, I had given my life to Him in a small church where my grandmother worshipped. But as I grew older and gained independence, I slowly took control back, convinced my plan was better than His.

That morning, it felt as though I had given up—not just on myself, but on my marriage and on life altogether. Right there on the side of the road, I finally called out to God. I said,

"God, I believe you're real. I don't fully understand this Christianity stuff, but if You can use this mess—here I am."

They weren't polished words. They were raw, honest, and desperate.

In that moment, I felt an overwhelming sense of relief. Nothing around me changed—my job was the same, my marriage was still broken—but something inside me shifted. A weight lifted. For the first time in years, I felt peace and clarity. Tears streamed down my face, not from sorrow, but from relief and joy. It was an emotion I hadn't experienced in a very long time.

That evening, I couldn't wait to share what had happened with my wife. I was excited, hopeful, and nervous all at once. But when I told her I had dedicated my life to following Christ, her response surprised me. She was skeptical and uncertain, especially since she hadn't grown up in church and didn't understand what being born again meant.

When I told her about my decision, she asked for a divorce.

I was stunned. I hadn't anticipated that response at all. I asked her how she felt about our relationship and whether she would be willing to try again. She expressed doubt, saying she didn't believe it would work.

I assured her that I would never force her to go to church or change her lifestyle. I made it clear that this was my personal decision. All I knew was that I could no longer build my life—or our marriage—without God as the foundation. I told her that while I was choosing to follow Christ, I deeply hoped she would remain part of my journey.

That moment marked the beginning of a new understanding: **what we build matters—but what we build on matters even more.**

Walking It Out Together

Beginning my journey with Christ was one of the most difficult seasons of my life. While surrendering to Him brought peace to my heart, it also introduced a profound sense of loneliness. Choosing to walk with God does not always mean pushing people away, but it can cause distance when those closest to you are not walking the same path. Even in those moments, I held on to the quiet assurance that I was never truly alone— God was with me.

As my relationship with Christ deepened, I felt an unexpected widening gap between my wife and me. I didn't know how to invite her into this new life without pushing her away. I wrestled with questions many spouses face: *How do I lead without forcing? How do I share my faith without creating resistance?*

One evening during prayer, I asked God directly how I could persuade my wife to walk this journey with me. I wondered if I needed to say more, do more, or convince her somehow. God's response was simple, yet deeply challenging: **"The only thing I want you to do is love her—no matter what."**

I questioned Him—*no matter what, Lord?* And again, the answer came clearly: **"Yes. No matter what."**

That moment marked a turning point. I chose to love my wife unconditionally, without expectation or agenda. For a while, nothing seemed to change on the surface. She treated me the same, and the distance remained. Yet something within me was changing. My love for her began to grow in ways I had never experienced before. I found myself expressing care, patience, and tenderness in new ways—without resentment and without pressure.

During that season, I prayed constantly—for her, for our marriage, and for my own heart. I asked God to reshape me, to teach me how to love the way Christ loves. I asked Him to make me a better husband, not through words, but through humility, consistency, and grace.

Over time, my wife noticed the change. One day, while we were sitting together at home on our day off, she looked at me and said words I will never forget: **"I want what you have."**

Then she asked, *"How do I get that?"* I told her simply, "Give your heart to God. He will take care of the rest."

She wanted to understand what that meant. When she asked, *"What does it mean to give your heart to Him?"* I responded with a question of my own: *"How did you trust your heart with me?"*

She had many questions, and I welcomed every one of them. I was filled with joy—not because I felt successful, but because I could see God gently working in her heart.

Eventually, she decided to come to church with me. That day is forever etched in my memory. After attending alone for so long, my best friend was finally beside me. Months of prayer were answered when she made the decision to give her life to Christ. When people ask her today what led her to faith, she often shares that it was the genuine transformation she saw in me that opened her heart to Jesus.

Once my bride came to know Christ, we felt as though we were beginning again. Although our foundation had been cracked for many years, we were given a fresh start. Before, without a blueprint, everything we built was fragile. Now, with Christ at the center of our marriage, we finally had something solid to build upon.

Our vision changed. Where we once felt lost, we now had direction. Our lives became centered on Christ, and instead of prioritizing ourselves, we learned to put Him first. That shift transformed our marriage. Love became less about demand and more about devotion. Growth no longer came through pressure, but through surrender.

This journey has not been easy. We still face difficult days and moments of tension. But on those days, we have learned to listen for God's voice rather than reacting to our own emotions or the whispers of the enemy.

Jesus said, *"My sheep hear My voice, and I know them, and they follow Me"* (John 10:27). This verse reminds us that hearing God's voice flows from relationship, not religion. Before we truly knew Him, sin and pride clouded our ability to discern His guidance. But through repentance and surrender, the Holy Spirit now lives within us, directing our steps.

The enemy is deceptive. He often disguises his lies as our own thoughts, seeking to destroy our marriages and our connection with God. That is why it is vital to remain anchored in Christ and rooted in Scripture. God's Word gives us clarity, discernment, and truth in the midst of confusion.

When Christ becomes the foundation, love is no longer something we strive to manufacture—it becomes something we receive and then give freely. And that kind of love has the power to restore even the most broken foundations.

Chapter Two Reflection

Chapter Two reminds us that marriage is more than a legal or social arrangement—it is a **divinely designed partnership**, reflecting God's image and purpose. True union involves recognizing and celebrating the unique strengths and perspectives each person brings. Differences are not obstacles but opportunities for growth, balance, and creativity.

Conflict and disagreements are inevitable, but handling them with patience, humility, and open communication allows couples to strengthen their bond rather than weaken it. Like building a home, a marriage requires a **solid foundation**, and Christ must be the cornerstone. Without Him, even the best intentions can crumble under pressure.

The chapter also emphasizes **the power of love rooted in God**: it transforms hearts, bridges gaps, and enables couples to navigate challenges without resentment. When marriage is built on Christ, love shifts from demand to devotion, from expectation to grace, creating a resilient, joyful, and lasting partnership.

Chapter Two Prayer

Heavenly Father,

Thank You for the gift of marriage and the divine design You have placed in it. Help us to see the unique strengths and differences in our spouse as blessings, not obstacles. Teach us patience, humility, and grace in times of disagreement, and guide us to resolve even the small "foxes" before they grow into larger problems.

Lord, be the foundation of our relationship. Let Christ's love flow through us, transforming our hearts and renewing our marriage daily. Help us to listen, support, and love each other unconditionally, trusting that with You at the center, our union will stand firm through every challenge. In Jesus' name, Amen.

Practical Takeaway

- *Build on Christ* – Make your marriage foundation strong by prioritizing God in your daily life. Pray together, study Scripture, and invite His guidance in decisions big and small.

- *Celebrate Differences* – Recognize that your unique traits complement your spouse. Use these differences to enhance teamwork, decision-making, and problem-solving.

- *Address "Little Foxes" Early* – Don't ignore small irritations; communicate openly and resolve them before resentment grows.

- *Practice Unconditional Love* – Love without expectation or control, reflecting Christ's patience and grace. Over time, this transforms both hearts and your relationship.

- *Seek Help When Needed* – Whether through mentors, pastors, or counseling, don't hesitate to gain wisdom and support to strengthen your marriage foundation.

chapter three

A SACRED COVENANT

*"For this reason a man shall leave his father and his mother,
and be joined to his wife; and they shall become one flesh."*

GENESIS 2:24

Marriage, in the framework of Scripture, is not merely a social contract or a legal arrangement—it is a **sacred covenantal bond**. This covenant transcends the simple union of two people. It embodies a deep, holy, and enduring commitment, one that a couple vows to uphold before God. Unlike a contract, which may reflect skepticism and serve a limited, transactional purpose, a covenant is built on trust, fidelity, and mutual devotion. It is spiritual, eternal, and reflective of the divine relationship between God and His people.

Historically, the weight of these vows was understood with profound reverence. The phrase *"until death do us part"* carried deep significance, symbolizing the unshakeable depth of commitment and the intention for a lifelong partnership. Today, however, the concept of covenant is often overlooked. Marriage is frequently perceived through a contractual lens rather than a sacred one. Prenuptial agreements, while sometimes practical, can unintentionally signal doubt or a lack of trust. This mindset may stem from past disappointments, fear of failure, or emotional wounds, but it also reflects a worldview that sees marriage as negotiable rather than enduring.

One of the greatest threats to a marriage's longevity is the presence of a **defeated mindset**. When one or both partners enter the union expecting struggle or failure, their thoughts can become strongholds that prevent the relationship from flourishing. A covenant, however, is meant to endure. It is not fragile, nor does it collapse at the first sign of difficulty. Storms will inevitably come—conflict, misunderstanding, external pressures—but the question is not whether challenges will arise; the question is **how the couple will emerge from them**. Will the experience strengthen the union, or allow it to wither?

The enduring strength of marriage is rooted in its covenantal nature, fortified when **Christ serves as the third strand** in the relationship. Ecclesiastes 4:12 illustrates this beautifully: *"A cord of three strands is not easily broken."* When God is woven into the fabric of the marital bond, He becomes the anchor for forgiveness, wisdom, purpose, and unwavering commitment. His presence allows couples to rise above selfish desires, fleeting human emotions, and relational pressures. Without Christ at the center, marriages are vulnerable to misunderstanding, unresolved conflict, and conditional love that cannot withstand the trials of life.

A covenantal marriage requires intentionality. It calls for **placing commitment to divine truth above human feelings**, for prioritizing the eternal over the temporal, and for seeking a love that mirrors Christ's selfless, sacrificial agapē love. In doing so, couples cultivate a marriage that is resilient, enduring, and reflective of God's eternal design.

In practical terms, a sacred covenant transforms marriage from a fragile, conditional arrangement into a **living, breathing partnership**. It reminds couples that their unity is not dependent on circumstances or emotions alone, but on the unchanging nature of God Himself. When Christ is the foundation, disagreements become opportunities for growth, trials become pathways to deeper intimacy, and love becomes steadfast, enduring, and transformative.

Marriage is not meant to be navigated alone or built on human effort alone. By embracing it as a **sacred covenant** anchored in Christ, couples can withstand adversity, experience true intimacy, and reflect God's glory through their lifelong commitment to one another.

A Servant's Heart

The Lord Jesus, fully God yet fully human, chose a path of humility and service rather than seeking honor or comfort for Himself. As Mark 10:45 reminds us: _"For even the Son of Man did not come to be served, but to serve, and to give his life as a ransom for many."_ From the very nature of His incarnation, Jesus embraced the posture of a servant, dedicating Himself sacrificially for the good of others.

On the night He was betrayed, just hours before the agony of the cross, His focus was not on His own suffering. He was fully aware of the trials that awaited Him—the betrayal, the abandonment, the excruciating pain. Yet, rather than retreat into self-preservation, His thoughts were on His disciples. He chose to demonstrate love not as an abstract concept, but as a lived reality—through humble, tangible action.

In John 13:4–5, we see Jesus taking on the role of the lowest servant in the household. "He got up from the meal, took off his outer clothing, and wrapped a towel around his waist. After that, he poured water into a basin and began to wash his disciples' feet, drying them with the towel that was wrapped around him."

This act was a profound expression of His love, demonstrating his commitment to His disciples until the very end. Even though He was about to be betrayed and abandoned by them, Jesus continued to love them deeply.

"Love is the greatest fruit that grows from a life surrendered to Christ. As we draw closer to Him, He begins to transform our hearts, teaching us to put the needs of others—especially our spouse—before our own.

In the everyday struggles of marriage, this love gives us patience when tempers flare, humility when pride rises, and grace when mistakes are made. It allows us to serve one another selflessly, not out of obligation, but from a heart shaped by Christ's own example. When love flows from Him, it becomes the steady foundation on which a marriage can flourish, even through trials and challenges."

In 1 Corinthians 13:4–8, Scripture offers a clear and searching picture of what love truly looks like. Love is patient and kind. It does not envy or boast, and it is not proud. It does not dishonor others or insist on its own way. Love is not easily angered, and it keeps no record of wrongs. It does not delight in evil but rejoices with the truth. It always protects, always trusts, always hopes, and always perseveres. Love never fails.

This is not a sentimental or convenient love. It is a selfless, enduring love—the very love that led Christ to the cross. His *agapē* love for humanity empowered Him to deny Himself completely and lay down His life for our sake. Jesus did not act out of obligation or emotion; He acted out of unwavering love.

This same kind of love is essential for a healthy, thriving marriage. Yet it is also important to acknowledge a difficult truth: we cannot produce this love on our own. Left to ourselves, we fall short. *Agapē* love grows only when we yield our hearts to the Holy Spirit, who is the true source of love within us. As we surrender control and invite God to work in us, He shapes our hearts to love the way Christ loves.

Scripture speaks directly to marriage in Ephesians 5. Husbands are called to love their wives as Christ loved the church—sacrificially, faithfully, and without reservation.

Wives are encouraged to submit to their husbands as the church submits to Christ—not out of fear or coercion, but from a place of trust and devotion to God. These instructions are not about power or hierarchy; they are about mutual surrender to Christ and mutual service toward one another.

Having a servant's heart goes far beyond the shallow or negative meanings often associated with the word *servant* in today's culture. In a world that prizes independence, self-promotion, and personal fulfillment, the call to serve can feel countercultural and even uncomfortable. Yet a servant's heart is not about weakness or loss of identity.

Embracing a servant's heart does not mean being diminished or controlled. Rather, it reflects a willing choice to love deeply, to serve wholeheartedly, and to put another's well-being before one's own comfort. It flows from empathy and compassion—a decision to set aside personal preferences in order to uplift and support another person.

When individuals live with a servant's heart, they demonstrate a quiet strength that resists the pull of selfishness. In a culture driven by individualism, this posture becomes a powerful witness. It reflects a deep understanding that relationships flourish not through self-interest, but through humility, generosity, and shared dependence on God.

In this way, a servant's heart is not a sign of subservience, but a testimony to the transforming power of Christ. It reveals how humility and sacrificial love can enrich both the one who gives and the one who receives.

When we dedicate our hearts fully to Christ, He begins to free us from our natural tendencies toward selfishness. Our human nature often leads us to protect our pride, pursue our own desires, or react harshly when we feel wronged. This might look like snapping at a spouse over something small, or holding onto resentment rather than extending grace. Christ invites us into a better way. He lifts us out of these cycles and teaches us to respond with love instead of defensiveness.

A close relationship with Him changes us over time. As we pray regularly, spend time in His Word, and listen for His guidance, we slowly begin to reflect His character. Jesus lived entirely for others. He gave His life freely, without seeking power or recognition. From Him flows true generosity—a generosity that softens our hearts and replaces selfishness with compassion.

This inner transformation cultivates a servant's heart within us. Jesus served without complaint, and we are invited to follow His example. In marriage, this looks like small but meaningful choices. A husband notices when his wife is weary and responds with care. A wife chooses forgiveness instead of resentment and offers encouragement instead of criticism. These acts may seem simple, but they carry profound spiritual weight.

When both spouses pursue this way of living, marriages grow stronger. Self-centered arguments lose their grip, grace becomes the prevailing atmosphere, and couples begin to flourish as they adopt the mind of Christ together. Families grow more united, and joy finds its place in the home.

You may be wondering where to begin. The answer is simple, though not always easy: surrender your heart to Jesus. Invite Him into the broken places. Allow Him to reshape your heart, and trust Him to do what you cannot do on your own. Transformation does not come from personal strength or effort—it comes from His. As you rely on Him, you will begin to see your relationships renewed by His love.

Threatened

One important truth to understand about the enemy of our souls is his deep hostility toward humanity and everything God has created for life and good. Scripture tells us plainly in John 10:10 that his aim is to steal, kill, and destroy. He stands in direct opposition to God's purposes, and wherever God brings life—both physical and spiritual—the enemy seeks to bring division and death.

Marriage, when aligned with God's design, is a powerful source of life. It nurtures love, unity, faith, and fruitfulness. Because of this, the enemy works relentlessly to prevent marriages from flourishing. He understands that if he can disrupt God's plan at its foundation, he can weaken what God intends to build through it.

Holy matrimony poses a real threat to the adversary precisely because of its divine origin. A marriage rooted in Christ reflects God's covenant love—faithful, enduring, and sustained by the Holy Spirit. When two people align their lives with God's purpose, their union becomes more than a human agreement; it becomes a living testimony of God's love at work in the world.

When a husband and wife are joined together in Christ, there is a spiritual strength present that goes beyond human effort. The enemy may attempt to strike at that bond through conflict, discouragement, or deception. Yet when a marriage is built on the solid foundation of Christ, it is not easily broken. In fact, the trials meant to weaken it often become the very means by which it grows stronger and more resilient.

This raises an important question—one that has echoed since the beginning of Scripture. Why did the enemy target the very first married couple? What kind of threat could a man and a woman, walking closely with God, possibly pose? The answer remains just as relevant today.

Marriage has always been central to God's design. In Eden, God established the union between Adam and Eve, declaring that the two would become one flesh. This sacred union points forward to Christ's love for His church—a love marked by faithfulness, sacrifice, and unity. From healthy marriages grow strong families, children grounded in faith, and homes that remain steady even in seasons of difficulty.

The enemy despises this kind of strength. Stable families limit his influence. Faith-filled homes pass down truth, nurture virtue, and create spaces where God's presence is known. When marriages are weakened or distorted, the ripple effects are felt far beyond the couple themselves.

We see this tension reflected in the culture around us, where marriage is often treated as temporary or optional, rather than sacred and enduring. When commitment is devalued and God's design is obscured, confusion and brokenness follow. These shifts slowly erode the understanding of marriage as a lifelong covenant, replacing it with something far less life-giving.

Yet marriage, as God intended it, speaks a powerful truth into the world. It declares that love can endure, that faithfulness is possible, and that life can emerge from the union of two people committed to one another and to God. The enemy, having lost his own place in God's presence, cannot recreate what he has forfeited. What he cannot possess, he seeks to undermine.

If your marriage feels threatened—by conflict, discouragement, or outside pressures—take heart. The very fact that it matters so deeply is a reminder of its value. What God has joined together, He is faithful to sustain. As you cling to Him, even in weakness, He continues to strengthen what the enemy works so hard to destroy.

Stay Strong

Disagreements will arise in every marriage. Conflict alone is not a sign of failure. What matters most is how a couple responds to those moments. When a husband and wife commit to praying together, seeking God together, and honoring the covenant they have made, their marriage is strengthened—

even through seasons of difficulty. A union rooted in Christ has the power to endure what might otherwise tear it apart.

This is what the enemy fears most: a marriage that remains faithful, united, and anchored in God. Holy matrimony reflects the beauty and order of heaven. When a couple stands firm together, their union becomes a living testimony of God's grace and faithfulness. For this reason, Scripture calls us to remain alert and vigilant. Your marriage matters far more than you may realize—it pushes back against darkness simply by standing strong.

The adversary is persistent and strategic. He understands that when families are weakened, the effects reach far beyond a single household. By attacking the family, he can influence communities, nations, and even generations. Homes are where our deepest relationships live—between spouses, parents, and children—and this is why the enemy so often targets them first.

Small cracks can quickly widen if left unattended. A misunderstanding turns into an argument. Hurt feelings go unspoken. Trust begins to erode. Love feels distant. Without care and intervention, a home that once felt safe can begin to feel fragile. The enemy thrives in these moments, whispering discouragement and sowing division where unity once lived.

The pain caused by a fractured marriage rarely stops with the couple alone. When families break apart, the emotional impact can ripple outward, affecting children and shaping how they view relationships, security, and love. These wounds can carry forward into adulthood, influencing decisions, behaviors, and futures. Strong families contribute to stable societies; broken homes often leave lasting scars.

History itself bears witness to this truth. Societies flourish when families are healthy and grounded, and they falter when the family structure erodes. When commitment weakens and responsibility is abandoned, the consequences extend far beyond individual choices. What begins in the home can eventually shape entire cultures.

Yet the enemy's reach goes even deeper. Scripture reminds us that eternity is at stake. When the foundation of a home is shaken, hearts can drift away from truth and hope. This is why the battle surrounding marriage is not merely emotional or relational—it is spiritual.

One of the adversary's most effective tactics is deception. He convinces us that conflict is purely personal, that it's only about our own pain, our own needs, our own happiness. He encourages us to believe that our choices affect no one else. Divorce can begin to look like an easy escape, a simple solution to deep wounds, without regard for its lasting impact.

Another common strategy is to convince us that our spouse is the enemy. Scripture speaks directly to this lie. Ephesians 6:12 reminds us that our struggle is not against flesh and blood, but against spiritual forces working behind the scenes. Your spouse is not your adversary—even when emotions run high and communication breaks down.

When harsh or accusatory thoughts arise—*They don't care. They're selfish. Why am I even trying?*—it's important to pause and recognize that not every thought deserves your agreement. Some thoughts are planted to divide, discourage, and harden hearts. They are not always rooted in truth.

This is where the mind of Christ becomes essential. As we grow closer to Jesus, He renews our thinking. The Holy Spirit gently brings clarity, helping us see situations more accurately and compassionately. Instead of assuming the worst, we begin to consider the full picture. Perhaps your spouse is overwhelmed, exhausted, or carrying unseen burdens. Grace opens space for understanding.

As our perspective shifts, so do our questions. Instead of asking, *Why aren't they meeting my needs?* we begin to ask, *How can I support them right now? What does love look like in this moment?* This change of heart does not ignore our own feelings, but it places them in God's care rather than allowing them to rule our responses.

God is faithful to guide us—not only in what to say, but when to say it. There are moments when silence and patience are acts of love, and moments when honesty needs to be shared gently and openly. The Holy Spirit helps us discern the right time—often in calm, unguarded moments—when hearts are more open and listening replaces defensiveness.

When couples choose to wait on God's timing, conversations become safer. Walls come down. Two hearts can meet again, sharing honestly and receiving one another with grace. In those moments, love is renewed—not because everything is suddenly perfect, but because Christ is present, doing what only He can do.

Staying strong does not mean never struggling. It means refusing to give up. It means standing together, even when the path feels uncertain, and trusting God to bring healing where it is needed most. As you remain anchored in Him, your marriage becomes not only a place of restoration for you, but a testimony of hope in a world that desperately needs it.

Strength In Unity

Love does not usually grow through grand gestures alone. More often, it develops quietly, one small step at a time. It begins with daily choices—choosing to put your spouse first in ordinary moments. It might look like washing the dishes late at night when you are exhausted, listening fully without interrupting, or choosing to forgive quickly after a painful word is spoken. These small acts may seem insignificant, but they carry great power.

Over time, consistent kindness ignites change. Hearts that once felt distant begin to soften. Walls built over years of disappointment and hurt slowly come down. What felt frozen begins to warm, and hope quietly returns.

In difficult seasons, stay strong. Hold on, even when it feels easier to let go. You are not alone in this work. God sees every effort that goes unnoticed and every sacrifice made in faith. In His perfect timing, He steps in with power and grace. He restores what once seemed beyond repair, heals old wounds within the home, and rebuilds trust where it has been broken. Love becomes more than words—it becomes visible, lived out, and deeply rooted.

God's work does not stop with your marriage. As He restores your relationship, others will take notice. Friends will see your perseverance and find hope for their own struggles. Families around you may be inspired by your commitment. Lives can be impacted because you chose to love when it was hard, to serve when it cost you something.

Believe it or not, this journey begins with you. This is where real action takes place. Each of us carries the effects of the fall—an inward pull toward selfishness that urges us to put ourselves first. We see it in everyday moments: choosing personal comfort over connection, responding sharply when kindness is needed, or prioritizing our own desires over the health of the relationship. Left unchecked, these habits quickly build walls between two hearts.

Selfishness has a way of turning us into victims. We begin to blame our spouse, telling ourselves, *They hurt me first.* Responsibility fades, and humility disappears. Rarely does anyone stop to say, *I contributed to this too.* Instead, excuses grow, pride swells, and blame shifts endlessly to the other person.

Unity cannot survive in this environment. Marriages often unravel not because of one major failure, but because of an ongoing cycle of blame. One accusation leads to another, and soon conflict becomes the norm. Healthy relationships require ownership—acknowledging your part, releasing the victim mindset, and choosing humility over pride.

If you truly desire healing and restoration in your marriage, it will require intentional effort. Someone has to lead the way. That means serving even when it's inconvenient, praying faithfully for your spouse, listening without preparing a defense, and loving without conditions. This work often costs tears, energy, and perseverance.

You should also be prepared for resistance. As you pursue unity, old wounds may resurface. Conflicts may feel more intense before they ease. Loneliness can feel sharper at times. The enemy does not easily surrender ground he has claimed. He may try to discourage you, distort your motives, or twist your efforts. Yet every prayer you pray and every act of love you choose weakens his hold. When you stand firm in Christ, ground is reclaimed.

True unity waits on the other side of surrender. Before unity can flourish, something within us must first be laid down. This is not a physical death, but a spiritual one—the surrender of ego, pride, and the insistence on our own way. The apostle Paul expressed this truth clearly in Galatians 2:20: *"I have been crucified with Christ."*

Jesus echoed this call in Matthew 16:24–25, teaching that anyone who desires to follow Him must deny themselves, take up their cross, and follow Him. In losing our lives for His sake, we discover true life. This is where faith becomes essential—trusting that God knows what we need even when surrender feels costly.

When you fully surrender to Christ, it is not a blind leap. The Holy Spirit assures us that God is trustworthy and faithful to meet our deepest needs. As we stop striving to fill our own emptiness, we find freedom and peace in Him.

As followers of Christ, we are called to give Him everything. In return, He takes what we surrender and breathes life into it. When a marriage is placed at the center of Christ's care, He reshapes it—redirecting hearts away from self-focus and toward sacrificial love for one another.

At first, surrender can hurt. It may feel like reopening wounds or letting go of long-held grievances. Choosing love over being right is rarely comfortable. Yet healing often begins right there—in the painful but freeing act of release.

Start small. Put gas in her car without expecting thanks. Forgive again, even when it feels unfair. Confess your faults first, as James 5:16 encourages. Serve quietly. Pray faithfully. These acts may feel unseen, but God uses them mightily.

God refines us through fire, and as He transforms us, our marriages begin to reflect that work. From surrender, unity grows. Amos 3:3 asks, *"Can two walk together unless they are agreed?"* Before we can walk well with our spouse, we must learn to walk faithfully with Christ.

For many years, we may have followed our own path, only to find confusion and discouragement at the end of it. Proverbs 14:12 reminds us that what seems right to us can ultimately lead to destruction. Apart from Christ, our hearts are easily misled.

Scripture also offers hope. Jesus taught that a divided house cannot stand. A united home, anchored in Him, not only endures but grows stronger. When we return to God's path and commit ourselves fully to it, our marriages do more than survive—they flourish under His loving guidance.

Chapter Three Reflection:

Marriage, as God designed it, was never meant to be fragile or disposable. It was created as a sacred covenant—one that reflects His own faithful, enduring love. As you reflect on this chapter, consider how easy it is to drift into viewing marriage through a worldly lens: focused on personal happiness, unmet expectations, or temporary emotions. Scripture calls us to something deeper.

A covenant does not deny hardship; it anticipates it. God knew that marriage would face conflict, disappointment, and seasons of strain. Yet He also provided a foundation strong enough to endure them all—His presence. When Christ stands at the center of a marriage, struggles are no longer signs of failure but invitations to grow in faith, humility, and love.

This chapter reminds us that marriage is both precious and contested. The very challenges you face may point to the value of what you hold. A marriage anchored in Christ becomes a place where sacrificial love is practiced, where forgiveness has room to breathe, and where unity is formed not by perfection, but by perseverance.

Take time to reflect honestly:

- Have you viewed your marriage more as a contract or a covenant?
- Where might pride, fear, or self-protection be creating distance?
- What would it look like to fully invite Christ into the difficult places?

God is not discouraged by weakness. He is drawn to surrender. When you offer Him your marriage—just as it is—

He faithfully begins the work of renewal.

Chapter Three Prayer:

Heavenly Father,

We come before You with humble hearts, acknowledging that our marriage belongs to You. You are the One who joined us together, and You alone are able to sustain what You have created.

Lord, forgive us for the times we have treated this sacred covenant lightly—when we have chosen selfishness over service, pride over humility, or distance over understanding. Search our hearts and reveal anything that stands in the way of unity.

Jesus, we invite You to be the center of our marriage. Teach us how to love as You love—patiently, sacrificially, and without condition. Where wounds remain, bring healing. Where trust has been broken, restore it. Where hope feels faint, breathe new life.

Holy Spirit, guide our thoughts, our words, and our actions. Help us recognize when conflict is not against one another, but part of a greater spiritual struggle. Give us discernment, grace, and strength to stand firm together.

We surrender our expectations, our rights, and our fears into Your hands. Shape our hearts into servant hearts. Make our marriage a reflection of Your covenant love—faithful, enduring, and full of grace.

We trust You, Lord. What You have joined together, let no force divide.

In Jesus' name, Amen.

Practical Takeaways:

- **Reaffirm the Covenant** - Set aside time—together or individually—to reflect on your marriage vows. Speak them aloud if possible. Remind yourselves that your commitment is not rooted in feelings alone, but in a promise made before God.

- **Practice One Act of Sacrificial Love Daily** - Choose one intentional act each day that puts your spouse first. It doesn't need to be grand—listen without interrupting, offer encouragement, complete a task without being asked. Let love be expressed through action.

- **Replace Blame with Ownership** - When conflict arises, pause before responding. Ask yourself: *What is my part in this?* Choose humility over defense. A simple phrase like, "I see where I could have done better," can shift the entire tone of a conversation.

- *Pray Together—Even Briefly* - If praying together feels difficult, start small. Hold hands and pray for one minute. Ask God for unity, wisdom, and protection over your marriage. Prayer invites God's presence into places words alone cannot heal.

- *Guard Your Thoughts* - Be mindful of internal narratives about your spouse. When critical or discouraging thoughts surface, ask God to help you see through His lens—one of compassion, truth, and grace.

- *Remember the Bigger Picture* - Your marriage matters— not only to you, but to your family, your community, and God's kingdom. Staying faithful in small, unseen ways has eternal significance.

Further Reflection:

Marriage is not an accident of circumstance, nor merely the result of human choice. It is sacred because God Himself is present within it. Long before you spoke your vows, God was already aware of the joys and the trials that would follow. Nothing you face now has taken Him by surprise.

THE KING & *His Bride*

God's true purpose for marriage

You may feel weary. You may feel unsure. You may even feel distant—from your spouse or from God Himself. Yet the covenant remains. God does not withdraw when love feels strained or when hope feels thin. He draws nearer.

A covenant is not sustained by perfection, but by faithfulness. It is upheld not by constant harmony, but by a willingness to return—to humility, to forgiveness, and to God. Even when words have failed and trust has been tested, the covenant still speaks. It declares that love can endure, that healing is possible, and that restoration is always within reach.

As you reflect on this chapter, release the pressure to fix everything at once. God does not ask you to rebuild your marriage in a single moment. He asks you to take the next faithful step. One prayer. One act of kindness. One decision to surrender your pride and choose love again.

Remember that you are not fighting alone. Christ stands within your marriage—not as a distant observer, but as the sustaining presence who strengthens what feels weak and breathes life into what feels broken. Where human strength ends, His grace begins. Let this truth settle in your heart: What God has joined together, He is committed to restoring.

chapter four

UNVEILING THE ENEMY'S PLAN

"The thief comes only to steal and kill and destroy; I have
come that they may have life, and have it to the full."

JOHN 10:10

Many of the struggles marriages face today cannot be fully understood without recognizing the spiritual reality behind them. Scripture teaches that there is an enemy who actively works against God's design for love, unity, and covenant. When couples are unaware of this reality, they often turn inward—blaming themselves or one another—without realizing that something external is also at work.

Understanding the role of Satan does not mean living in fear or suspicion. Rather, it equips couples with clarity. When we recognize that some pressures are not merely personal or emotional, but spiritual, we can respond differently. Awareness allows us to stand together instead of turning against one another. It helps us resist division and face challenges with wisdom, humility, and shared strength.

Scripture reveals that Satan was not created evil. He was formed as a magnificent being—an exalted archangel identified as Lucifer—endowed with beauty, authority, and proximity to God (Ezekiel 28:13–15; Isaiah 14:12). Yet pride took root in his heart. Instead of honoring God, he desired glory for himself. That pride led to rebellion, and rebellion led to his fall.

God expelled him from heaven, and Scripture tells us that many angels followed him in that rebellion (Revelation 12:4). From that moment on, Satan set himself against everything God loves and everything God creates for good. His mission became one of opposition—distorting, dismantling, and destroying whatever reflects God's nature and purposes.

The Bible makes clear that Satan knows his time is limited. Revelation 12:12 speaks of his fury, fueled by the knowledge that his end is coming. This urgency intensifies his efforts. Humanity, made in the image of God and invited into relationship with Him, becomes a primary target of his rage. Jesus Himself exposed the enemy's intent plainly: *"The thief comes only to steal and kill and destroy."* Satan's hatred is not random—it is deeply personal. He once stood in God's presence and lost everything through pride and deception. What he forfeited, he can never regain. And because he cannot destroy God, he seeks to wound God by attacking what God loves most.

Marriage occupies a central place in God's design. It reflects covenant, unity, faithfulness, and sacrificial love. Scripture reveals marriage as a living picture of Christ's relationship with His Church. Because of this, marriage becomes a strategic target in the enemy's plan.

Satan rarely attacks marriages all at once. Instead, he works subtly and patiently. Pride begins to creep in. Selfishness gains ground. Small disagreements grow unresolved. Communication weakens. Temptation presents itself as relief. Over time, what once felt secure begins to feel fragile.

These patterns directly oppose God's intention for marriage. God designed marriage to be a place of safety, growth, forgiveness, and shared purpose. When marriages fracture, the damage often extends beyond the couple—affecting children, families, communities, and even future generations.

This reality can feel heavy, but it is not meant to discourage. It is meant to awaken discernment. Satan's influence is real, but it is not ultimate. He is active, but he is not victorious. His power is limited, and his defeat is already assured through Christ.

Strong marriages disrupt his plans. When couples forgive instead of retaliate, pray instead of withdraw, and choose unity over pride, they resist the enemy's influence. In doing so, they reflect heaven's values on earth—love over fear, truth over deception, grace over condemnation.

Resilient marriages become quiet testimonies of God's faithfulness. They shine light into darkness. They remind the world that covenant love is possible, healing is real, and God's design still stands.

If your marriage feels under pressure, take heart. Awareness is not a sign of defeat—it is the beginning of strength. When couples face the battle together, anchored in Christ, they are far more powerful than they realize. What the enemy intends to destroy, God is more than able to redeem.

Forbidden Fruit

From the beginning of Scripture, temptation has often appeared in the form of something desirable, promising fulfillment while quietly leading away from God's design. In marriage, the enemy uses a similar strategy. He does not usually arrive with obvious destruction, but with subtle invitations—small compromises that seem harmless at first, yet slowly unravel trust and unity.

Within the sacred tapestry of marriage, these temptations can take many forms. Lustful thoughts and fantasies may arise, offering excitement, escape, or novelty outside the covenant. In today's world, social media and digital spaces often become fertile ground for these struggles. What begins as a casual interaction or innocent conversation can gradually shift into emotional dependence. Boundaries blur. Comparisons creep in. Attention meant for one's spouse is quietly redirected elsewhere.

Discontentment is another common doorway. It often disguises itself as unmet needs or unfulfilled dreams. The enemy whispers questions that stir restlessness: *Is this all there is? Don't you deserve more? Look at what others have.* These comparisons feed dissatisfaction and erode gratitude, causing spouses to view one another through a lens of lack rather than grace.

Isolation further weakens a marriage's defenses. When couples withdraw from supportive community—trusted friends, church fellowship, spiritual accountability—they become more vulnerable. God designed us to grow and persevere together. When that support is absent, temptations often feel louder and more persuasive.

Adultery is often viewed as the ultimate betrayal of marriage, yet it rarely begins with a conscious decision to be unfaithful. Even strong, committed Christian marriages are not immune. The enemy is patient and observant, waiting for moments of fatigue, loneliness, or emotional neglect.

Often it begins innocently. A coworker listens attentively. A friend seems to understand more deeply. An emotional connection forms that feels affirming and safe. This "forbidden fruit" glimmers with the illusion of intimacy— someone who appears more present, more compassionate, more affirming than one's spouse in that moment.

In seasons of vulnerability, hearts longing for connection can become open to these lies. The enemy subtly reframes reality, suggesting that one's needs are not being met at home or that fulfillment must be found elsewhere. Over time, attention shifts, boundaries erode, and what once seemed unthinkable begins to feel justified.

Often, these temptations take hold where intimacy has weakened. A lack of emotional, spiritual, or physical connection can create distance marked by loneliness, resentment, or misunderstanding. When couples stop sharing their hearts and their lives fully, a gap forms—and that gap will seek to be filled.

For Christian couples, healing begins not with dramatic gestures, but with a return to the foundations.

Prayer comes first - Praying together invites God back into the center of the relationship. It fosters spiritual intimacy and shared dependence on Him. Prayer softens hearts, encourages vulnerability, and creates space to share struggles and hopes honestly before God and one another.

Communication must follow - Healthy intimacy requires honest, gentle conversation. This means listening without defensiveness and speaking without accusation. Setting aside intentional, distraction-free time to talk allows emotional distance to close and understanding to grow.

Shared experiences matter - Reconnecting through simple activities—walking together, preparing meals, laughing over a shared hobby—helps restore joy. These moments remind couples that companionship is not lost; it is waiting to be rediscovered.

Physical affection also plays a role - Non-sexual touch—holding hands, hugging, sitting close—rebuilds safety and warmth. These small gestures communicate care and presence, often opening the door for deeper connection over time.

Wise support can strengthen the process - Counseling, pastoral care, or trusted church resources offer guidance, accountability, and perspective. Seeking help is not a sign of failure; it is an act of humility and commitment to restoration.

As couples navigate the complexities of marriage, vigilance is essential—but so is hope. Temptation thrives in secrecy and silence, but it loses power when brought into the light. Open communication, prayerful awareness, and intentional connection form strong defenses against the enemy's schemes.

True love is not found in fleeting excitement or false intimacy. Its beauty lies in faithfulness—choosing one another daily, even when it requires effort and patience. By anchoring your marriage in Christ, nurturing honest dialogue, and remaining attentive to one another's hearts, you can resist the allure of the forbidden and rediscover the richness of covenant love.

When trust, love, and accountability shape a marriage, temptation no longer defines the story. Instead, couples learn to savor the lasting fruit of commitment—the deep joy, security, and intimacy that grow when two people walk faithfully together before God.

Forgive One Another

Unforgiveness acts like a heavy anchor in a marriage. It keeps hearts tied to past pain and prevents couples from moving forward into the life God desires for them. Jesus warned of this danger when He taught that looking back can keep us from fully following Him (Luke 9:62). In marriage, unresolved hurts create emotional barriers that stifle intimacy, communication, and growth. When wounds are left unaddressed, they do not remain neutral—they quietly shape how spouses see one another and how they respond in the present.

Each refusal to forgive is not merely a reaction to pain; it is a decision that keeps resentment alive. While unforgiveness may feel like self-protection, it ultimately harms the one who holds onto it. Bitterness takes root, trust erodes, and suspicion replaces tenderness. Over time, love struggles to breathe in an atmosphere weighed down by unresolved hurt.

Forgiveness, though deeply challenging, is essential for healing and renewal. Letting go of past offenses does not minimize the pain or excuse wrongdoing. Rather, it opens the door for restoration and allows couples to engage fully with one another again. When forgiveness is embraced, it creates space for understanding, growth, and renewed connection. It frees both hearts from the prison of the past and invites God's healing presence into the present.

Some transgressions cut far deeper than others. Betrayals—particularly those that violate trust—leave lasting scars. When trust is broken, the foundation of the relationship feels unstable, and the memory of the hurt can linger like a shadow over every interaction. Without healing, that pain can quietly transform love into resentment and closeness into emotional distance.

If left unresolved, this kind of hurt does not fade with time alone. Instead, it can harden into bitterness that poisons communication and drains joy from the relationship. Moments that once carried warmth become tense. Hope feels fragile. The marriage begins to suffer under the weight of unspoken pain.

Healing from such wounds requires more than endurance—it requires surrender. Turning to Jesus becomes essential. In His presence, couples can find both the courage to forgive and the strength to heal. Forgiveness, in this sense, is not only for the one who caused the pain, but also for the one who carries it. It releases the burden that no heart was meant to bear alone.

At some point, a choice must be made: to cling to bitterness or to place the hurt in Christ's hands. Choosing surrender does not erase the past, but it allows God to redeem it. Through forgiveness, reconciliation becomes possible—not necessarily as a return to what once was, but as the birth of something new. Trust, though different, can be rebuilt with honesty, boundaries, patience, and grace.

Forgiveness is not rooted in fleeting emotion. It is an act of faith—often repeated many times—especially when feelings lag behind obedience. Scripture never suggests that forgiveness is easy, nor does it promise that healing happens overnight. But it does assure us that renewal is possible through Christ.

When we surrender our pain to Him, we open our hearts to transformation. What once felt like a dead end can become a place of growth. Each step toward forgiveness becomes a steppingstone toward renewal, aligning us with God's promise that we are being made new.

Forgiveness also invites a new perspective. Rather than allowing pain to define the future, it allows God to reshape it into a testimony of grace. Through Christ's strength, grudges lose their grip, and compassion takes their place. What once divided begins to heal.

God promises this kind of transformation. In Ezekiel 36:26, He speaks of giving His people a new heart and a new spirit. This promise points to deep, spiritual renewal—one that enables forgiveness beyond human ability. Such forgiveness is not produced by willpower alone; it is a work of the Holy Spirit, softening hearts and empowering love where bitterness once lived.

A renewed heart cultivates humility, grace, and understanding. It allows spouses to see one another not only through the lens of pain, but through the lens of redemption. In marriage, this new heart becomes essential for restoring trust and intimacy. Forgiveness becomes the thread that weaves healing back into the covenant.

Ultimately, the journey toward healing and renewed love is inseparable from forgiveness. It is a gift made possible through Christ, one that restores relationships and deepens our walk with God. As forgiveness takes root, wounds are transformed into wisdom, scars into testimony, and broken places into evidence of God's restoring grace.

In choosing to forgive, couples do not deny the pain they have endured—they declare that pain will not have the final word. Christ does.

Confusion

Scripture teaches us that God is not the author of confusion, but of peace. Confusion, therefore, is one of the enemy's most effective and subtle tools. When allowed to take root in a marriage, it clouds judgment, distorts communication, and slowly pulls two hearts apart. What often begins as misunderstanding can quietly escalate into discouragement, resentment, and, if left unchecked, even the breakdown of the relationship.

Confusion creates havoc wherever it is allowed to linger. We see its effects in workplaces, communities, and even among nations—miscommunication gives way to conflict, and conflict can spiral into destruction. The same pattern unfolds within the home. When confusion settles into a marriage, it breeds arguments, fuels emotional distance, and replaces peace with tension.

Many people do not realize that confusion is rarely neutral. Scripture warns that where confusion exists, all kinds of disorder and harmful behavior can follow. At its core, confusion is often less about intelligence or logic and more about the heart. It grows when we stop seeking to understand one another and instead focus on defending our own position.

One of the first signs that confusion has entered a marriage is the breakdown of true listening. Hearing words is not the same as listening from the heart. When couples stop listening with empathy and openness, walls begin to rise. Those walls block clarity, and communication becomes strained. Conversations that once brought understanding now end in frustration.

Instead of approaching one another with curiosity and humility, spouses may come armed with assumptions—believing they already know what the other is thinking or intending. Each person becomes convinced that their perspective is the correct one, that their version of events is the truth. In doing so, they forget an essential reality: there are often two experiences in a conflict, and true truth is found in Christ, not in winning an argument.

When the Holy Spirit is not intentionally invited into the home and into conversations, confusion quickly fills the space. Scripture tells us that it is the Holy Spirit who leads us into all truth. Without His guidance, we rely solely on our own thoughts, emotions, and interpretations—which are often influenced by fear, past wounds, and pride. It is only when we choose to listen to the Spirit rather than our internal narratives that we begin to see through the fog of confusion.

When confusion is allowed to settle into the heart, it does not remain passive. Over time, it erodes reason, patience, and peace. Healthy dialogue becomes difficult. Small disagreements feel overwhelming. What once could be resolved with a calm conversation now escalates into emotional standoffs.

Confusion operates like a stronghold. It is not merely a moment of misunderstanding but a pattern the enemy uses to keep couples stuck. To confront and overcome it, surrender is required—not once, but daily. Each day presents a choice: to rely on our own understanding or to submit our hearts and wills to Christ.

Choosing clarity requires intentionality. It means deciding to listen with the heart of Christ, especially when emotions are heightened. When invasive or accusatory thoughts arise—thoughts that speak against your spouse or distort their intentions—you are invited to pause and resist them. Standing firm does not always mean speaking immediately; often, it means choosing restraint, prayer, and discernment.

The enemy rarely begins with chaos. Confusion often starts small—a minor misunderstanding, an unclear comment, a poorly timed conversation. If left unaddressed, that small confusion can snowball into a larger conflict. A simple request becomes an argument. A neutral statement feels like criticism. Both individuals walk away hurt, misunderstood, and more distant than before.

Ironically, many couples desire the same outcome. They want peace, connection, security, or progress—but confusion twists communication so that those shared desires feel opposed rather than aligned. Instead of working together, spouses find themselves working against one another.

God created men and women with differences—not to divide them, but to complement one another. These differences were designed to bring balance, creativity, and strength to marriage. When sin and spiritual opposition distort these differences, what was meant to bless becomes a source of frustration and emotional strain. The beauty of partnership is replaced with tension.

Yet this distortion is not permanent. When couples choose to listen with humility, patience, and the mind of Christ, confusion loses its power. Understanding begins to grow. Conversations soften. What once felt like conflict becomes an opportunity for connection.

Clarity in marriage is not achieved by being right—it is achieved by being surrendered. When both spouses commit to inviting the Holy Spirit into their conversations, decisions, and reactions, peace begins to return. Confusion fades in the presence of truth, and truth is always accompanied by love.

Choosing clarity means slowing down, asking questions instead of making assumptions, and seeking understanding rather than control. It means remembering that your spouse is not your enemy, even when communication is strained. Together, under the guidance of Christ, what once felt chaotic can become ordered, and what once felt hopeless can be restored.

God delights in bringing peace where confusion has reigned. As couples submit their hearts to Him, He faithfully replaces chaos with clarity and restores unity where division once stood.

Neglect

In today's fast-paced world, it can feel like a miracle that anything meaningful gets done at all. Life moves quickly. Schedules overflow. Responsibilities stack up. Ironically, many of the tools created to make life easier—technology, instant communication, constant access—have done the opposite. Instead of freeing our time, they often consume it.

Busyness has become our new normal. With countless apps, notifications, and demands competing for our attention, we are more connected digitally than ever before—yet often less present relationally. Social media promised connection, but too often it has left us distracted, inward-focused, and emotionally unavailable to the people closest to us.

One of my first pastors once said, *"A friend does not have time; a true friend makes time."* That truth applies to every relationship, but especially to marriage. Time is not something we stumble upon—it is something we choose. What we prioritize reveals what we truly value.

When a spouse feels neglected, the damage goes far deeper than hurt feelings. Neglect creates wounds that affect the emotional, mental, physical, and even spiritual well-being of a person. Over time, it erodes trust, intimacy, and safety within the marriage. What was once vibrant slowly begins to wither.

God has given us vivid examples of this reality in creation. A plant that is neglected—deprived of water, sunlight, and care—does not remain neutral. It dies. Animals that experience prolonged neglect often become fearful, withdrawn, or aggressive. Their behavior is shaped not by who they were created to be, but by what they lacked.

The same is true in marriage. A neglected spouse may grow distant, anxious, resentful, or emotionally guarded—not because they stopped caring, but because something essential has been missing for too long.

Most neglect is not intentional. It rarely begins with disregard or indifference. Instead, it often starts with good intentions and delayed promises: *"If I can just get through this season... If I can land this promotion... If I can finish this project, everything will settle down."*

This is a familiar lie—one that nearly all of us have believed at some point. One hour turns into five. One task leads to another. And before we realize it, the people we love most have been receiving only what's left of us, not the best of us.

Even as I write, I am keenly aware of this tension. Creative work, ministry, and responsibility can quietly demand more than they should. Without intentional boundaries, even good things can cause harm. We must continually realign our priorities so that those we love are not unintentionally sidelined.

We wear many hats in life—parent, provider, leader, mentor, friend. These roles matter. But before all of them, if we are married, we are first the spouse of one.

Our work, hobbies, pets, friendships, and even our children must not take precedence over our marriage. And yes, this includes ministry. Not God—but ministry. God must always come first. But ministry is not God, and when ministry replaces marital faithfulness, something has gone terribly out of order. God's design is clear: **God first, spouse second, everything else follows.**

When we confuse this order, we unintentionally create space for the enemy to work. Misplaced priorities often become open doors to disconnection, resentment, temptation, and emotional distance.

Consider the story of Adam and Eve. Scripture tells us that Eve was approached by the serpent—but where was Adam? The Bible does not say he was far away, yet his silence and passivity speak volumes. Neglect does not always look like absence; sometimes it looks like being nearby but disengaged.

There are many "snakes" today—distractions, temptations, emotional substitutes—waiting patiently for moments of neglect. We are called to guard what God has entrusted to us, and that begins by being present, attentive, and invested in our spouse.

What we once admired, pursued, and cherished must continue to be protected. When we stop nurturing what we worked so hard to gain, we risk losing it.

Scripture gives us a sober warning in Proverbs 24:33–34, "A little sleep, a little slumber, a little folding of the hands to rest— and poverty will come on you like a thief."

This principle applies not only to work, but to relationships. A little neglect here. A little distance there. Over time, the marriage becomes emotionally bankrupt—not because of one major failure, but because of prolonged inattention.

Yes, life carries real responsibilities. Bills must be paid. Work must be done. Children must be cared for. But how we prioritize within those responsibilities is a choice.

Marriage does not thrive by accident. What we pour into it is what we will receive in return. Attention nurtures connection. Presence builds safety. Intentional love restores intimacy.

Neglect may feel small in the moment, but its effects are lasting. The good news is that restoration often begins the same way—with small, intentional choices. Time given. Attention restored. Love re-centered.

Without doubt, God, who honors covenant, blesses every sincere effort to return to what matters most.

Chapter Four Reflection

Chapter Four invites us to step back and see our marriage through a wider, more honest lens. It reminds us that not every struggle we face is simply the result of personality differences, unmet expectations, or poor communication—though those are real. Scripture reveals that there is also a spiritual dimension at work. An enemy exists who actively opposes covenant, unity, forgiveness, clarity, and faithfulness.

This awareness is not meant to instill fear, but clarity. When couples misunderstand the nature of the battle, they often turn on one another instead of standing together. Hurt becomes blame. Confusion becomes accusation. Distance becomes justification. But when we recognize that our spouse is not the enemy, something shifts. Unity becomes possible again.

Throughout this chapter, we have seen how the enemy works patiently and subtly—through temptation, unforgiveness, confusion, and neglect. Rarely does he destroy a marriage in a single moment. More often, he erodes it through small compromises, unaddressed wounds, misplaced priorities, and silence. Yet we have also seen something far more powerful: the redemptive strength of Christ working through humble, surrendered hearts.

Marriage matters deeply to God. It reflects His covenant love, His faithfulness, and His design for life and flourishing. That is why it is so fiercely opposed—and why it is so worth fighting for. Strong marriages resist darkness not by perfection, but by dependence on Christ. They forgive when it's hard. They choose clarity over confusion. They guard against neglect. They remain faithful when temptation whispers otherwise.

If your marriage feels weary, strained, or under attack, let this chapter be an invitation—not to despair, but to awareness and renewal. What the enemy seeks to destroy, God longs to restore. Where confusion has reigned, God offers peace. Where neglect has taken root, God invites renewed attention. Where unforgiveness has hardened hearts, God offers a new heart.

Victory does not begin with fixing everything at once. It begins with seeing clearly, surrendering honestly, and choosing to stand together under Christ's authority. When couples do that, the enemy's plans are exposed—and his power begins to crumble.

Chapter Four Prayer

Heavenly Father,

We come before You with humble hearts, acknowledging that without You, we are easily confused, distracted, and wounded. Thank You for revealing truth through Your Word and for shining light on the spiritual realities that affect our marriage. Lord, we confess that there have been moments when we turned against one another instead of turning to You. Forgive us for the times we allowed pride, selfishness, unforgiveness, confusion, or neglect to take root in our hearts and our home.

We recognize now that our spouse is not our enemy. Jesus, we invite You into the center of our marriage again. Where temptation has whispered lies, speak truth. Where wounds remain open, bring healing. Where confusion has clouded our understanding, restore clarity and peace. Where neglect has caused distance, renew our desire to love intentionally and sacrificially.

Holy Spirit, guard our hearts and minds. Teach us to listen—to You and to one another. Give us discernment to recognize the enemy's tactics and courage to resist them together. Help us to forgive as we have been forgiven, to love as You have loved us, and to remain faithful in both joy and difficulty.

We place our marriage under Your authority. What the enemy has tried to steal, kill, or destroy, we ask You to redeem. Restore hope where it has faded, unity where it has been fractured, and joy where it has been lost.

We trust You, Lord. We choose You. And we commit our covenant to You once again.

In Jesus' name, Amen.

Practical Takeaway

- *Name the Battle Correctly* - The next time conflict arises, pause and ask: *Is my spouse really the enemy—or is something else at work here?* This simple shift can prevent blame and open the door to unity.

- *Invite God Into the Tension* - Don't wait until things are calm to pray together. Even short, honest prayers in the middle of struggle invite the Holy Spirit to bring clarity and peace.

- *Guard Against Small Compromises* - Temptation rarely starts big. Pay attention to subtle shifts—emotional distance, unchecked thoughts, blurred boundaries, or growing secrecy—and address them early.

- *Practice Daily Forgiveness* - Forgiveness is not a one-time act. Ask God daily to soften your heart and release lingering resentment before it takes root.

- *Choose Clarity Over Assumptions* - When confusion arises, slow down. Ask questions instead of making assumptions. Seek understanding rather than control.

- *Reorder Your Priorities* - Examine where your time and energy go. Ask honestly: *Does my spouse receive my best or what's left?* Small changes in attention can produce deep restoration.

- *Stand Together* - Unity is one of the greatest threats to the enemy's plans. Even when you disagree, commit to standing side by side under Christ's leadership.

chapter five

THE BATTLES OF MATRIMONY

"Be completely humble and gentle; be patient, bearing with one another in love. Make every effort to keep the unity of the Spirit through the bond of peace."

EPHESIANS 4:2-3

Stress comes in many forms—some loud and overwhelming, others quiet and persistent. When the weight of responsibilities, expectations, and unresolved pressures begin to pile up, it does not take much to upset the balance. A single added burden can feel like the final straw. In these moments, stress does not remain contained; it spills over into our homes and into our marriages.

Jesus speaks directly to this reality in Matthew 6:34 when He tells us not to worry about tomorrow. This invitation is not a call to neglect our responsibilities or disengage from life. Rather, it is a loving call to rest—resting not in avoidance, but in trust. Christ invites us to release the burden of control and place our confidence in His faithful care.

Resting in Christ begins with surrender. It is choosing to trust that when we invite Him into our circumstances, He will lead us along a path marked by peace rather than exhaustion, clarity rather than chaos. Left to ourselves, we often carry stress in unhealthy ways—internalizing it, suppressing it, or unintentionally releasing it through frustration and impatience toward our spouse.

When stress goes unchecked, it becomes a breeding ground for tension and conflict within a marriage. Small disagreements escalate quickly. Communication becomes strained. Joy fades, and unity weakens. This is one of the subtle ways the enemy works—using pressure and fatigue to divide what God intends to strengthen.

Throughout this chapter, we will bring light to some of the everyday battles married couples commonly face—the recurring arguments, misunderstandings, and pressures that can quietly erode connection if left unaddressed. These struggles are not signs of failure, but invitations to grow.

Ultimately, the responsibility rests with each of us to respond differently. Healing begins when we choose to lay down pride, release anger, confront unforgiveness, and seek a better way forward. Lasting change does not start with our spouse changing—it begins with surrender. As we place every burden, every frustration, and every fear into the hands of Christ, He faithfully begins the work of restoration within us and within our marriage.

The main conflict in marriages:

Communication - One of the most common sources of conflict in marriage is communication. Many struggles arise not from a lack of love, but from poor listening, misunderstandings, or the avoidance of difficult conversations.

In ancient Israel, the shofar was used to communicate important messages—calling people to worship, signaling war, or announcing retreat. Each message was understood by its distinct sound and tone. In the same way, communication within a marriage depends not only on words, but on tone, timing, and intent. When the message is unclear, confusion follows.

Effective communication often marks the difference between growth and breakdown in a relationship. Whether we realize it or not, we are always communicating. Even silence sends a message. Over time, however, unresolved hurts and unspoken frustrations can distort communication, turning misunderstanding into a harmful pattern. Walls are built, clarity is lost, and the ability to move forward together becomes increasingly difficult.

Without clear and loving communication, it is impossible to walk in unity. This is why inviting the Holy Spirit into our conversations is essential. He helps filter our words and soften our hearts, transforming our message from *"I don't hear you"* or *"I don't care"* into *"I hear you, I understand you, and I love you."*

In John 10:27, Jesus says, *"My sheep hear My voice; I know them, and they follow Me."* With these words, Jesus makes it clear that relationship produces recognition. Those who truly know Him are not confused by His voice—they recognize it because they are familiar with Him.

The same principle applies in marriage. When spouses know one another deeply and walk in close relationship, communication becomes clearer. Words are less easily misunderstood, and intentions are not quickly taken as offense. Familiarity breeds understanding, not confusion. Just as we recognize the voice of Christ through intimacy with Him, we learn to understand our spouse's heart when we truly know them.

Sex & Intimacy - Few areas of marriage are as deeply personal—or as easily misunderstood—as sex and intimacy. Differences in desire, frequency, expectations, or preferences can quietly become sources of tension and hurt if they are not handled with wisdom, grace, and humility. Because intimacy touches the heart, the body, and the soul, it is also one of the areas the enemy most frequently targets.

Scripture speaks clearly and lovingly to this subject. In 1 Corinthians 7:5, Paul writes, *"Do not deprive one another except perhaps by mutual consent and for a time, so that you may devote yourselves to prayer. Then come together again so that Satan will not tempt you because of your lack of self-control."* This passage reveals two important truths: intimacy matters to God, and prolonged disconnection creates vulnerability. Physical closeness within marriage is not selfish or sinful—it is protective, unifying, and sacred.

Proverbs 5:18–19 echoes this design, encouraging husbands to *"rejoice in the wife of your youth."* God's Word affirms that delight, desire, and enjoyment belong within the covenant of marriage. Sex was never intended to be a burden or bargaining tool; it is meant to be a source of joy, bonding, and mutual giving.

At the same time, this subject must be approached with care, because men and women often experience intimacy differently. Many women feel loved primarily through emotional connection. When insecurity, exhaustion, unresolved conflict, or emotional distance is present, physical intimacy can feel difficult or unsafe. Withdrawal is often not rejection, but a sign that something deeper needs attention.

Men, on the other hand, often experience love and affirmation through physical connection. When intimacy is absent, they may feel unwanted, unloved, or disconnected—even if their spouse cares deeply. Without understanding one another's needs, both partners can end up feeling rejected, lonely, and misunderstood.

This disconnect often happens not because love is absent, but because love is being expressed in different languages. When couples have not learned how the other experiences love, both may give sincerely—and still miss one another entirely.

This is why intimacy in marriage must go deeper than the physical or emotional alone. True marital intimacy begins spiritually. When Christ is at the center of the relationship, He aligns hearts before bodies. A shared spiritual connection creates safety, understanding, and unity that naturally flows into emotional closeness—and eventually into physical intimacy.

When couples pray together, worship together, and invite Christ into their daily lives, something shifts. Emotional walls begin to soften. Compassion grows. Misunderstandings are handled with grace rather than defensiveness. In this environment, physical intimacy becomes an expression of unity rather than a source of pressure or pain.

Sex is not merely a physical act—it is a gift from God, given to be enjoyed within marriage between a husband and a wife. While it includes procreation, it was never limited to that purpose alone. God designed sexual intimacy to create a bond unlike any other—to make two people "one flesh." It is one of the most powerful expressions of unity on earth and a sacred reflection of Christ's relationship with His Church.

Because this gift is so powerful, the enemy works relentlessly to distort it. He offers counterfeits—false intimacy that promises fulfillment but delivers brokenness. Lust, adultery, and other distortions attempt to separate what God intended to unite. The enemy cannot create anything new; he can only twist what God has already declared good.

This is why guarding intimacy in marriage matters so deeply. Protecting it requires intentional time, honest conversation, emotional care, and spiritual leadership. Flames do not stay lit without tending. Connection does not deepen without effort. Yet when couples choose to prioritize one another and center their intimacy in Christ, what once felt strained can be restored.

Where spiritual intimacy grows, emotional intimacy is strengthened. Where emotional intimacy is nurtured, physical intimacy becomes life-giving rather than burdensome. And where Christ reigns, counterfeit intimacy loses its appeal.

Sex and intimacy were never meant to divide a marriage. When surrendered to God's design, they become one of His most beautiful tools for unity, healing, and deep, abiding love.

Money & Finances - Few subjects create as much tension in marriage as money. Differences in spending habits, approaches to saving, views on debt, and long-term financial goals can quickly turn into ongoing conflict if they are not addressed with wisdom and unity. Finances are not merely practical concerns—they are deeply connected to trust, security, control, and fear. Because of this, they often become a battleground in marriage.

Scripture speaks clearly about money, not because God is concerned with wealth itself, but because He cares about the condition of our hearts. The Bible repeatedly calls us to be good stewards of what we have been entrusted with. Proverbs 21:20 reminds us that *"the wise store up choice food and olive oil, but fools gulp theirs down."* Wisdom in finances means living within our means, planning carefully, and resisting the urge to consume impulsively.

Financial strain often begins when one or both spouses spend more than they earn. At first, it may seem manageable— a credit card here, a loan there—but over time, debt accumulates and pressure builds. When financial stress increases, patience decreases. Conversations about money become emotionally charged. Small purchases spark arguments. Anxiety replaces peace. The enemy is quick to exploit this strain, using financial pressure to sow division, blame, and resentment between spouses.

When there is no shared financial vision, money becomes a constant source of conflict. Without clarity, every expense feels personal. One spouse may feel controlled, while the other feels burdened. Trust erodes, and unity weakens. This is why agreement and transparency are essential. Financial peace is rarely accidental—it is the result of intentional planning and mutual cooperation.

A clear and shared financial plan is one of the strongest defenses against financial turmoil. This plan must involve both husband and wife. Finances should never be handled in isolation, secrecy, or imbalance. Marriage calls for partnership, and stewardship is no exception.

There is an old saying: *"If you fail to plan, you plan to fail."* Scripture affirms this principle while also reminding us where our true security lies: *"A person plans his course, but the Lord directs his steps"* (Proverbs 16:9). Planning is our responsibility; direction belongs to God.

A healthy financial plan begins with honesty. Couples should clearly identify what is coming in each month, what debts exist, what expenses are fixed, and what can realistically be set aside for savings. This includes bills, groceries, transportation, and discretionary spending. When everything is placed in the light, fear loses power and clarity begins to grow.

Once a plan is established, boundaries can be set. Couples can decide together how much discretionary spending is reasonable and how to handle larger purchases. These agreements protect unity and prevent unnecessary conflict. They also replace assumptions with understanding.

Yet the most important part of any financial plan is not the numbers—it is prayer. Finances should never be separated from faith. When couples pray together over their finances, they acknowledge God as their provider, not money. Inviting God into financial decisions shifts the focus from fear to trust, from scarcity to stewardship.

Scripture reminds us that God multiplies what is surrendered to Him. What feels insufficient in our hands becomes abundant in His. When finances are placed before God in prayer, He brings wisdom, restraint, creativity, and provision in ways we could never orchestrate on our own.

The Bible also warns that *"where there is no vision, the people perish."* The same is true in marriage. Without a shared financial vision, couples drift toward stress and conflict. With vision—rooted in faith, wisdom, and unity—finances become a tool rather than a weapon.

Money was never meant to divide a marriage. When handled with humility, planning, and prayer, it becomes an opportunity for teamwork, trust-building, and spiritual growth. As couples learn to steward together, they often discover that financial peace is not just about having more—it is about walking together under God's guidance.

When Christ leads your finances, fear loosens its grip, unity grows stronger, and even limited resources become enough.

Children & Parenting - Few responsibilities test a marriage like raising children. Decisions about discipline, values, education, routines, and boundaries can quickly become sources of tension—especially when spouses come from different family backgrounds. Each parent brings their own experiences, expectations, and wounds from how they were raised. What felt normal in one household may feel foreign or even wrong in another. Without unity, these differences can turn parenting into a battleground rather than a shared calling.

Parenting was never meant to be carried by one spouse alone. God designed children to be raised through partnership. When one parent shoulders the responsibility while the other withdraws—or when parents openly disagree in front of their children—the family structure weakens. Children thrive not when parents are perfect, but when they are united.

Both a mother and a father bring essential, God-given strengths to the raising of children. A mother often reflects nurturing, tenderness, and emotional connection. A father often reflects stability, guidance, and healthy discipline. These roles are not rigid or exclusive, but complementary. Together, they form a balanced picture of love and leadership. When these strengths work together rather than against each other, children experience safety, clarity, and consistency.

Conflict arises when parents undermine one another—correcting each other in front of the child, sending mixed messages, or competing for authority. This not only confuses children, but it also places unnecessary strain on the marriage. Parenting is most effective when decisions are discussed privately, prayed through together, and presented with unity.

Discipline, in particular, requires agreement. Children need boundaries that are loving, consistent, and clear. When discipline is inconsistent or driven by emotion rather than wisdom, children become confused or fearful. Discipline is not about punishment—it is about instruction, protection, and guiding a child toward maturity.

Values also shape the heart of parenting. Decisions

about diet, schooling, friendships, media, faith practices, and daily routines all reflect deeper beliefs. Without intentional conversation and shared vision, parents can find themselves pulling in opposite directions. Unity does not mean identical thinking—it means shared direction.

Scripture gives clear guidance in this area: "Train up a child in the way he should go, and when he is old he will not depart from it." This instruction is not a guarantee of perfection, but a promise of influence. Children learn most not from what they are told, but from what they observe. A home marked by love, unity, prayer, and mutual respect leaves a lasting imprint.

Raising children in the way of the Lord begins with parents who are themselves submitted to Him. When husband and wife seek God together, their parenting gains clarity. Decisions are no longer driven by fear, comparison, or pressure, but by prayer and discernment.

Children do not need flawless parents—they need present ones. They need parents who are willing to listen, to correct with love, to apologize when wrong, and to stand together. A united marriage provides a secure foundation from which children can grow into confident, compassionate, and faithful adults.

Parenting is not simply about raising children; it is about shaping future generations. When couples choose unity over control, partnership over pride, and prayer over reaction, they reflect God's design for family. And in that unity, children are given the greatest gift of all—a home grounded in love, truth, and faith.

Household Chores - Household responsibilities may seem small compared to other marital challenges, yet they are among the most common sources of daily tension. Laundry must be done, dishes need washing, meals need preparation, grass must be cut, and the home requires ongoing care. When these responsibilities are unclear or unevenly shared, frustration can quietly build and eventually spill over into conflict.

God did not design marriage to function through unspoken expectations. One of the healthiest practices a couple can establish early on is a clear and honest "road map" for managing the household. This may include creating a shared chore list, dividing responsibilities evenly, or rotating tasks on a weekly or seasonal basis. The method matters less than the agreement. What brings peace is clarity.

Listening to one another is essential in this area. Each spouse carries different responsibilities outside the home—

work demands, studies, parenting duties, ministry, or caregiving roles. Being mindful of one another's schedules and energy levels allows couples to extend grace rather than keep score. A healthy marriage is not built on rigid fairness, but on mutual consideration.

Scripture calls believers to serve one another in love: *"Serve one another humbly in love"* (Galatians 5:13). Household responsibilities become acts of worship when they are done with a servant's heart. Contributing to the home is not merely about completing tasks; it is about honoring one another through practical care.

Christ Himself modeled servant leadership. Scripture reminds us that *"the greatest among you will be your servant"* (Matthew 23:11). Husbands are called to love their wives as Christ loved the Church—sacrificially and selflessly (Ephesians 5:25). That kind of love is expressed not only in words, but also in action, often in the ordinary and unseen moments of daily life.

While traditional teachings have often emphasized distinct household roles, a growing and biblically grounded understanding of marriage encourages flexibility, teamwork, and responsiveness to one another's needs. Chores are not simply gendered duties; they are opportunities to love. When couples view shared responsibility as partnership rather than obligation, resentment gives way to appreciation.

A marriage thrives when both spouses ask not, "Is this my job?" but, "How can I serve you today?" When burdens are shared, the home becomes a place of peace rather than pressure.

This list of challenges is not exhaustive, but it highlights some of the most common areas where conflict arises in marriage. The key to preventing these issues from becoming daily battles is simple, though not always easy: place the Lord first, listen with humility, remain mindful of one another, and commit to working together.

When a couple chooses to bless rather than burden one another, even the smallest tasks become sacred. In serving one another faithfully, marriages reflect the heart of Christ—and unity grows where division once tried to take root.

Chapter Five Reflection

Marriage is not effortless, but it is worth fighting for. Challenges—stress, miscommunication, finances, parenting, and daily responsibilities—do not define it. When Christ is at the center, struggles become opportunities for unity. Marriage thrives not through control, but through love, patience, humility, and faith, as couples stand together before God.

Chapter Five Prayer

Heavenly Father,

We come before You acknowledging that marriage is both a gift and a responsibility. You see the pressures we carry, the misunderstandings we face, and the places where stress has weighed heavily on our hearts. We confess that at times we have responded out of frustration rather than faith, pride rather than humility, and fear rather than trust.

Lord, we invite You into every area of our marriage. Teach us to rest in You when life feels overwhelming. Help us to communicate with grace, to listen with compassion, and to speak with love. Where intimacy has been strained, restore connection. Where finances have caused fear, bring wisdom and peace. Where parenting has created tension, give us unity and discernment. Where daily responsibilities have felt burdensome, teach us to serve one another joyfully.

We lay down pride, unforgiveness, and self-centeredness at Your feet. Fill us with Your Spirit, that we may be patient, gentle, and kind toward one another. Strengthen our bond, guard our unity, and help us to reflect Christ in our marriage.

We trust You with our hearts, our home, and our future.

What feels heavy to us, we place in Your capable hands.

In Jesus' name, Amen.

Practical Takeaway

- *Schedule Sacred Time Together* - Set aside intentional, distraction-free time each week to connect— emotionally, spiritually, and practically. Even short, consistent moments build intimacy and understanding.

- *Pray Together Regularly* - Prayer realigns hearts. Begin with simple prayers if needed. Inviting God into your conversations and decisions creates unity and softens conflict.

- *Address Issues Early, Not Emotionally* - Small misunderstandings grow when ignored. Choose calm, honest conversations before frustration has time to harden.

- *Create Shared Plans* - Whether it's finances, parenting, or household responsibilities, clarity reduces conflict. Make decisions together and revisit plans as seasons change.

- *Serve One Another Daily* - Look for practical ways to ease your spouse's load. Acts of service—no matter how small—communicate love louder than words.

- *Fight the Real Enemy Together* - Remember that your spouse is not the enemy. Stress, pressure, and division are. Stand united, not divided.

- *Choose Progress Over Perfection* - Growth in marriage happens through faithfulness, not flawlessness. Celebrate small victories and extend grace when mistakes happen.

Final Encouragement

The battles of matrimony are not meant to break you—they are meant to refine you. When Christ leads your marriage, every challenge becomes an opportunity for deeper unity, stronger love, and greater testimony. What you surrender to Him, He faithfully redeems.

chapter six

OVERCOMING THE ENEMY'S LIES

"Be sober-minded; be watchful. Your adversary the devil prowls around like a roaring lion, seeking someone to devour."

1 PETER 5:8

The enemy of our souls is the ultimate deceiver—the father of lies (John 8:44). His strategy is cunning: he rarely speaks outright falsehood. Instead, he mixes a lie with a portion of truth, making it appear convincing and harmless. This was exactly how Satan deceived Eve in the Garden of Eden.

In Genesis 3:1-5, the serpent approached Eve, questioning God's command regarding the tree of the knowledge of good and evil. He told her that she would not die if she ate the fruit. Technically, this was true—she would not die physically—but he left out the most critical part: disobedience would bring spiritual death, separation from God. By presenting only part of the truth, Satan made the lie believable.

This is how he still works today. He tempts us through our desires, exploiting the parts of truth that appeal to us while hiding the consequences (James 1:14). The initial temptation may seem harmless or even pleasurable—an innocent conversation, a minor compromise—but sin often works like a slowly constricting snake, wrapping itself around your life. Little by little, it tightens its grip, injecting poison that damages relationships, peace, and your spiritual life.

The aftermath of falling for a lie is always heavier than the initial pleasure. Regret, guilt, broken trust, and lasting consequences are what the enemy never reveals. A harmless decision can quickly spiral into destructive patterns if not recognized and resisted early.

Satan's lies are insidious, but they are not stronger than the truth of God's Word. Every word he speaks is a distortion, a trap designed to steal joy, weaken marriages, and destroy homes. The key to overcoming his schemes is vigilance and obedience:

- *Stand firm in God's Word* - Know His promises and commands. Truth is your strongest defense.

- *Guard your marriage* - Protect your relationship with your spouse by fostering trust, transparency, and unity.

- *Protect your home* - Cultivate a spiritual atmosphere of prayer, worship, and accountability, leaving no room for deception.

When we recognize the enemy's tactics, we can resist him. When we speak truth, set boundaries, and stay anchored in God, the lies lose their power. Sin may appear enticing, but its consequences are always far greater than its appeal. Christ provides the strength, wisdom, and discernment we need to see through the lies and walk in freedom.

Stand Your Ground

The enemy is relentless in his attacks, and marriage is one of his primary targets. This truth is not meant to instill fear, but alertness. Awareness equips us to defend what God has entrusted to us. A nonchalant attitude, however, leaves the door open for deception and destruction.

Consider the example of King David. In 2 Samuel 11:1, we read that David remained in Jerusalem during the spring—a time when kings were expected to go to war. By neglecting his responsibilities and leaving his guard down, he fell into sin, committing adultery with Bathsheba. How many times have we, like David, allowed the enemy to ensnare us simply because we let our guard down?

Standing your ground is not about fear; it's about vigilance. The Word of God provides both a strategy and a promise. In 1 Corinthians 10:13, we are reminded: *"No temptation has overtaken you except what is common to mankind. And God is faithful; he will not let you be tempted beyond what you can bear. But when you are tempted, he will also provide a way out so that you can endure it."*

This scripture reassures us that God not only limits the power of temptation, but He also provides a clear path to victory. We are never left defenseless.

One of the ways God equips us is through the Armor of God (Ephesians 6:10-17). This armor is both defensive and offensive. We are commanded to:

- Stand firm in truth with the belt of God's Word.
- Protect our hearts with righteousness.
- Prepare our feet with the gospel of peace.
- Carry faith as a shield to quench fiery attacks.
- Wear salvation as a helmet to guard our minds.

- Wield the sword of the Spirit, which is the Word of God.

Ephesians 6:10-13 reminds us that our battles are not against flesh and blood, but against spiritual forces of darkness. After equipping ourselves with this armor, God commands us to **stand our ground**. Not temporarily, not halfheartedly, but steadfastly.

Standing firm is not a one-time event. Marriage, like life, has seasons of rest and seasons of battle. Even in peaceful seasons, vigilance is essential. We fight not out of anger, but out of love—for our spouse, our children, and our home. Even when we are weary, we cannot give up; often, breakthroughs come immediately after our greatest battles.

Nehemiah provides a powerful example. While rebuilding the walls of Jerusalem, he faced constant opposition. Yet, in Nehemiah 4:14, he encouraged the people: *"Don't be afraid of them. Remember the Lord, who is great and awesome, and fight for your families, your sons and daughters, your wives and your homes."*

As we rebuild our marriages, God calls us to the same stance. Stand firm. Fight for your family. Trust Him. Watch what He will do.

It's also important to recognize why the enemy attacks. He doesn't waste his energy on what is irrelevant or weak. He targets what threatens him. If your marriage is strong, God-centered, and a reflection of His love, it becomes a threat to the enemy. That is why he attacks. The good news is that God is greater than any scheme, temptation, or assault the enemy can devise.

Standing your ground is a posture of faith. It is a daily commitment to resist deception, protect your marriage, and walk in the victory Christ has already won for you. The battle may be long, but victory is sure for those who refuse to relinquish what God has entrusted to them.

God Has Called You for Such a Time

God is a God of order, intention, and purpose. If you are a child of God, then your life—and your marriage—are not accidents. They are not random, insignificant, or misplaced. One of the enemy's most effective lies is convincing couples that their marriage was a mistake, that it holds no meaning, and that it would be better abandoned than fought for. The truth of Scripture tells a very different story.

Every person who belongs to Christ has an appointed place in the Kingdom of God, and every marriage centered in

Him carries divine purpose. Your marriage was not only formed by love—it was formed with intention. You have been called, and your union has been positioned for something greater than you may yet see.

Even when a marriage feels broken, worn down, or beyond repair, God sees it through the lens of redemption. He desires to use what the enemy intended for harm as a testimony of His grace and restoring power. Scripture reminds us that when we do not give up, we will reap a harvest in due season. Our responsibility is not to control the outcome, but to trust the process and remain faithful.

The story of Esther beautifully illustrates this truth. Esther was an orphaned Jewish girl living in Persia, raised by her cousin Mordecai. By every outward measure, her life seemed insignificant. She came from a place of loss and obscurity. If judged by her beginnings, no one would have expected her to change history. Yet God had already written her story.

Esther was chosen to become queen of Persia under King Ahasuerus. At the appointed moment, God used her position to save an entire people from annihilation. When a wicked official named Haman plotted genocide against the Jews, Esther was called to act. Approaching the king without invitation meant risking her life, yet she chose courage over comfort. Through her obedience, the enemy's plan was exposed, Haman fell, and God's people were delivered.

Mordecai's words to Esther still echo through Scripture and into our lives today: *"Who knows whether you have come to the kingdom for such a time as this?"*

This truth applies not only to individuals, but to marriages.

You may not see it now, but God has placed your marriage where it is for a reason. What feels like a season of struggle may actually be a season of preparation. God's Word assures us in Jeremiah 29:11 that He knows the plans He has for us—plans for good and not for harm, plans to give us hope and a future.

Walking by faith means trusting God beyond what we see or feel. It means anchoring our hope in His promises rather than our circumstances. Even when a marriage appears lifeless, God specializes in resurrection. When surrendered to Him, no marriage is beyond restoration.

God is calling your marriage for such a time as this. Just as Esther was raised up during a season of despair, God is raising up Christian marriages to shine as light in a broken world. We live in a culture that has lost faith in marriage and its sacred purpose. Many have been deeply wounded, disillusioned, and weary. True love is questioned. Commitment is doubted. Divorce has become common—even within the church.

Yet this is precisely why restored marriages matter so deeply.

Those who have endured hardship, faced the storm, and experienced God's healing are living testimonies of His faithfulness. Your story—marked by perseverance, forgiveness, and grace—has the power to offer hope to others who believe all is lost.

God restores what seems ruined. He revives what appears dead. And He uses redeemed marriages as witnesses to His unchanging truth: that love can endure, covenant still matters, and nothing is beyond His ability to heal.

You and your marriage are not overlooked. You are not forgotten. You have been called—for such a time as this.

Being a Blessing not a Burden

Marriage was never designed to be a place where one spouse drains the other. God's design is that husband and wife become a source of strength, encouragement, and blessing to one another. While no one is perfect, Scripture gives clear guidance on what it looks like for both men and women to walk in godliness within marriage—and what happens when they do not.

A Godly Man: A Source of Strength and Safety - In 1 Corinthians 16:13–14, the apostle Paul offers a powerful exhortation that outlines the character of a godly man: *"Be watchful, stand firm in the faith, act like men, be strong. Let all that you do be done in love."*

Within these two verses, we see five defining traits of a man who becomes a blessing to his home rather than a burden.

Be watchful - A godly man remains spiritually alert. As the priest and spiritual leader of the home, he takes responsibility for the atmosphere he allows into his life and his family. This includes guarding what influences the home—conversations, entertainment, attitudes, and beliefs.

He does not lead passively, but intentionally filters what enters his heart and household. His life sets the example his spouse and children will follow.

Stand firm in the faith - A man cannot lead spiritually if he is not rooted spiritually. Standing firm begins with a personal relationship with God—time in Scripture, consistency in prayer, and obedience to God's Word. When a man is grounded in Christ, he becomes a stable foundation rather than an unstable force within the marriage.

Act like men - The phrase "act like men" comes from the Greek and carries the meaning of courage, maturity, and responsibility. Biblical manhood is not defined by dominance or aggression, but by accountability and strength of character.

As Paul writes in 1 Corinthians 13:11, maturity requires leaving childish ways behind. Godly men grow up, take responsibility, and lead with wisdom rather than impulse.

Be strong - True strength is not arrogance or self-confidence— it is humility and self-control. Scripture reminds us, *"Let him who thinks he stands take heed lest he fall"* (1 Corinthians 10:12).

A godly man acknowledges his weaknesses and relies on the Spirit of God for strength. Temptation itself is not sin; yielding to it is. Real strength is exercised when a man submits himself to the Spirit's control rather than his own desires.

Let all that you do be done in love - Love is the anchor that holds everything together. Without love, leadership becomes harsh, discipline becomes cruelty, and conviction becomes condemnation.

Godly men love deeply—Jesus first, then their wife, their children, the Word of God, and the people of God. This love is expressed not only through words, but through gentleness, patience, and presence.

Ephesians 5:25 commands husbands to love their wives as Christ loved the Church—sacrificially and selflessly. Love must be spoken and demonstrated. A man who leads without love becomes militant rather than godly.

Jesus Himself is the ultimate model of manhood. God became flesh and experienced fatigue, rejection, misunderstanding, temptation, and suffering—yet He remained faithful. Jesus was strong without being harsh, courageous without being cruel, and loving without compromise.

He overcame every temptation, showing us that godly strength is possible through surrender to God.

In contrast, a man who lacks vigilance, neglects his faith, avoids responsibility, or lives for himself becomes a burden to his home. Where there is passivity, selfishness, or unchecked pride, instability follows. Such a man does not protect the home—he exposes it.

A Godly Woman: A Builder of Her Home - For women, Scripture offers a clear and inspiring model in Proverbs 31. The Proverbs 31 woman is not defined by perfection, but by godly character. She is described as noble, capable, wise, and God-fearing. She strengthens her household through diligence, kindness, and discernment. Her confidence is rooted in the Lord, not in appearance or comparison.

She is a blessing because she builds rather than tears down. Her words bring life. Her actions bring peace. Her faith anchors her family. She manages her responsibilities with wisdom and carries herself with quiet strength.

Scripture also presents a contrast.

Proverbs 14:1 states, *"The wise woman builds her house, but with her own hands the foolish one tears hers down."* This verse reveals how deeply our choices affect the atmosphere of the home. A woman who walks in wisdom creates stability, while one driven by foolishness—contention, bitterness, or pride—slowly dismantles what God desires to build.

Proverbs further warns about the destructive power of constant conflict: *"Better to live on a corner of the roof than share a house with a quarrelsome wife"* (Proverbs 21:9).

A quarrelsome wife is like the constant dripping of a leaky roof in a rainstorm (Proverbs 27:15).

These verses are not meant to shame, but to caution. Constant contention, nagging, or unresolved anger can drain the life from a marriage just as surely as neglect can. Harmony does not mean silence—it means wisdom in speech and humility in conflict.

Choosing to Be a Blessing - Being a blessing rather than a burden is a daily choice. It requires humility, self-examination, and submission to God's design. Both husband and wife are called to build, protect, and nurture what God has entrusted to them.

When men lead with courage and love, and women build with wisdom and grace, marriage reflects the heart of God. In such a home, burdens are shared, strength is multiplied, and God's presence is evident.

A godly marriage does not happen by accident. It is built intentionally—one faithful choice at a time.

Overcoming

Scripture tells us that we are not unaware of the enemy's schemes (2 Corinthians 2:11). And yet, despite this awareness, many of us still find ourselves falling into the same traps—

repeating the same arguments, reacting in the same unhealthy ways, and wondering why change feels so slow. We ask ourselves hard questions: *Why do I keep failing? Why do I respond this way in my marriage? Why does progress feel so difficult?*

The apostle Paul wrestled with these same frustrations. In Romans 7, he openly admits the inner conflict that exists within every believer: *"For I do not do the good I want to do, but the evil I do not want to do—this I keep on doing."* Yet Paul does not end in despair. He points us to the answer—Jesus Christ. Christ is not only our Savior; He is our daily strength, our help, and our deliverer.

The Christian walk is not a single moment of victory— it is a daily journey. Scripture describes this process as moving "from glory to glory." We have not yet reached perfection, but when we are in Christ, something within us changes. Our desires begin to shift. What once felt natural begins to feel wrong. What once controlled us slowly loses its grip.

Overcoming does not always happen overnight. Growth often looks gradual. There are days when we still struggle with sharp words, defensiveness, impatience, or the urge to retaliate. Yet as we continue walking with Jesus, those moments begin to lose their frequency and power. What once provoked an argument may eventually be met with silence, grace, or understanding. This is evidence of transformation at work.

The longer we walk with Christ, the more our hearts begin to reflect His. Our thinking changes. Our reactions soften. Our responses become less driven by emotion and more guided by wisdom. The old patterns of the flesh are slowly replaced by the life of the Spirit. We are no longer who we once were—and we are not yet who we will be—but we are being made new.

For a marriage to grow and thrive, this transformation must be intentionally applied. Love, patience, kindness, peace, and self-control are not optional—they are essential. The fruit of the Spirit must be practiced, even on the days we do not feel like it. Especially on those days. Feelings come and go, but obedience produces lasting fruit.

Overcoming in marriage means choosing grace over reaction, humility over pride, and peace over proving a point. It means responding with love even when it feels undeserved. These choices are not signs of weakness; they are evidence of spiritual maturity.

Scripture also reminds us of an important truth: our struggle is not against flesh and blood. Our spouse is not the enemy. The real battle takes place in the spiritual realm. This is why worldly solutions alone will always fall short. The weapons we fight with are not carnal, but spiritual—made powerful through God to tear down strongholds.

Strongholds in marriage often take the form of habits, mindsets, and unresolved wounds—patterns of communication, cycles of anger, or deeply rooted fears. These are not broken through willpower alone, but through surrender, prayer, and reliance on Christ.

Revelation 12:11 declares how believers overcome the enemy: *"They overcame him by the blood of the Lamb and by the word of their testimony; they did not love their lives so much as to shrink from death."* Victory begins with what Christ has already done—the blood of the Lamb. It continues as we testify to His work in our lives and choose obedience over self-preservation.

Overcoming is not about never failing—it is about refusing to quit. It is about getting back up, turning again to Christ, and trusting that He is faithful to complete the work He began. When Jesus is our source, failure does not define us. Grace does.

A marriage centered on Christ is not free from battles, but it is never without hope. In Him, healing is possible. Change is real. And victory—step by step—is assured.

Chapter Six Reflection

We are reminded that the battles faced in marriage are rarely accidental—they are often rooted in deception. The enemy's greatest weapon is not force, but lies that sound reasonable, subtle, and even harmless. When believed, these lies slowly weaken trust, unity, and purpose. Yet Scripture assures us that awareness brings power. When truth is known and Christ is placed at the center, deception loses its grip.

This chapter also reveals that overcoming is not about perfection, but perseverance. God has not called marriages to merely survive attacks, but to stand firm, grow stronger, and become testimonies of His restoring power. Whether through vigilance, godly leadership, mutual encouragement, or daily surrender, victory is possible when couples choose to fight for one another instead of against one another.

Ultimately, overcoming the enemy's lies requires faith, humility, and intentional obedience. When spouses commit to being a blessing rather than a burden, to standing their ground in truth, and to trusting God's purpose for their marriage, they reflect Christ to a watching world. What the enemy intends to destroy, God delights in restoring.

Chapter Six Prayer

Heavenly Father,

We thank You for the truth of Your Word and the light it brings into our lives and marriages. We acknowledge that we are often tempted, distracted, and vulnerable—but You are faithful. Forgive us for the times we have believed lies, lowered our guard, or allowed fear and frustration to lead our responses.

Today, we choose to stand firm. We place the full armor of God upon our hearts, our minds, and our marriage. Help us to recognize deception quickly and respond with truth, wisdom, and love. Teach us to be a blessing to our spouse—to speak life, extend grace, and lead with humility.

Strengthen us for the battles we face. Restore what has been damaged. Renew what feels weak. And use our marriage as a testimony of Your power, faithfulness, and redemption. We trust You, Lord, and we surrender all to You. In Jesus' name, Amen.

Practical Takeaway

This week, commit to one intentional action that strengthens truth and unity in your marriage.

- Identify one lie or unhealthy pattern that has influenced your marriage (miscommunication, fear, resentment, passivity).
- Replace it with truth from Scripture and a godly response.
- Pray together—even briefly—asking God to guard your hearts and align your actions with His will.
- Choose one way each day to be a blessing to your spouse through words, service, or encouragement.

Small, consistent acts of obedience create lasting change. When truth guides your steps and Christ leads your marriage, the enemy's lies lose their power—and victory becomes a daily reality.

THE ULTIMATE LOVE STORY

"And over all these virtues put on love, which binds them all together in perfect unity."

COLOSSIANS 3:14

The greatest love story has never been written in a novel, performed on a stage, or captured on a screen. The greatest love story is written in the pages of Scripture. It is a love that bleeds, a love that saves, and a love that never wavers. It is not driven by emotion or convenience, but by covenant. This is the love of God.

From Genesis to Revelation, the Bible tells one continuous story of love—God pursuing a people who continually turn away from Him. Knowing humanity would reject Him again and again, God still chose love. He laid aside His divine privilege, stepped into human flesh, endured rejection, suffering, and death, and paid the ultimate price for a bride who had wandered far from Him. He did not do this out of obligation, but out of love—an immeasurable, sacrificial love meant to restore what was lost.

Scripture repeatedly portrays God as a faithful Bridegroom pursuing an unfaithful bride. One of the most striking examples of this is found in the book of Hosea. Through Hosea's painful marriage to his unfaithful wife, Gomer, God illustrates His unwavering love for Israel despite their continual idolatry and betrayal. Hosea's story is not merely a tragic relationship—it is a living picture of God's heart.

Gomer's unfaithfulness ultimately leads her into slavery. Yet the most powerful moment of the story is not her failure, but Hosea's response. He goes to the slave market and buys back the very woman who betrayed him. He redeems her, restores her, and brings her home—not as a servant, but as his wife.

This is the Gospel.

In the same way, we were sold into bondage because of sin. We wandered, rejected God's love, and pursued our own desires. Yet Christ went to the cross—our slave market—and paid the price for our freedom. Despite our repeated rejection, He redeemed us and called us His own once again. This truth should deeply challenge how we view marriage.

How many times have we rejected our spouse—not always through physical unfaithfulness, but through neglect, indifference, selfish priorities, or hardened hearts? How often have we chosen our own comfort, desires, or pride over love? And yet, many of us hold onto resentment for minor offenses that happened years ago, unwilling to forgive even as we have been forgiven.

Scripture leaves no room for excuses. Ephesians 4:32 calls us to "be kind to one another, tenderhearted, forgiving one another, as God in Christ forgave you."

God forgave us when we did not deserve it. Grace, by definition, is undeserved favor. It is forgiving even when it feels unjustified. This kind of grace is not weakness—it is strength rooted in love. When practiced in marriage, grace nurtures healing, restores trust, and strengthens the bond between husband and wife. Grace does not excuse sin, but it chooses restoration over rejection.

Another beautiful picture of redemption is found in the book of Ruth. Set during the time of the Judges, Ruth tells the story of a Moabite widow who chooses loyalty, faithfulness, and obedience over self-preservation. Though she belonged to a people outside of God's covenant, Ruth placed her trust in the God of Israel. Through her faithfulness, God led her to Boaz, her kinsman-redeemer, who redeemed her and brought her into his family.

This story points beyond itself to God's greater plan of redemption. Ruth's lineage leads directly to King David, and ultimately to Jesus Christ. It is a powerful reminder that God redeems those who were once outsiders and makes them His own.

This is agape love—selfless, sacrificial, and unconditional. It is not natural to us; it must be cultivated through surrender to God. The love that heals marriages is not human effort alone, but divine love flowing through yielded hearts.

If we desire redemption and healing in our marriages, it must begin with us individually. Before love can be fully lived out horizontally with our spouse, it must be received vertically from God. When we allow His love to transform us, it reshapes how we forgive, how we serve, and how we remain faithful—even when it is difficult.

Marriage, at its core, is meant to reflect this ultimate love story. A love that redeems. A love that forgives. A love that restores. And when Christ is at the center, what once seemed broken can be made whole again.

Rekindle the Flame

Who does your spouse's heart belong to today? For some, that question brings fear, regret, or sorrow. You may find yourself thinking, *It's too late. I've lost her... I've lost him. There's no way to rebuild what we've torn down.* The damage feels too deep, the distance too great.

But the truth is this: it is never too late for God.

Rekindling a marriage does not happen overnight, and it does require time, patience, and sincerity. Yet when the desire for restoration is genuine and persistent, God is faithful to walk with you through the process—step by step, moment by moment. This was true in my own marriage.

After about ten years, my wife and I were barely holding on. If you could even call it that, we were hanging by a thread. We had become strangers—roommates living under the same roof, sharing space but not life. Emotionally, we had given up on one another. Or at least, that's what we told ourselves. In reality, we still cared deeply, but pain had taught us to build walls for protection. Those walls made it easier to survive—but impossible to love.

Change did not come quickly, and it certainly did not come easily. It began the day I surrendered everything to God. Even then, I had no idea what the outcome would be. I didn't know if my wife would be willing to try again, or if the damage was already beyond repair. From my perspective, we had hurt each other too deeply. It felt impossible.

But surrender always opens the door for God to work. As I gave my life fully to Christ, something began to change within me. Slowly, quietly, but unmistakably, God started transforming my heart. My love for my wife was rekindled— not as a return to what once was, but as something deeper and stronger than before. God gave me a greater love for her than I had ever known, one rooted not in emotion, but in commitment and grace.

There were moments when I grew impatient. I wanted quick results. I wanted visible change in my marriage right away. But God used those moments to teach me patience—to trust the process rather than rush the outcome. Restoration, I learned, is rarely instant. It is built through consistency, humility, and faithfulness.

Jesus speaks to this principle in Revelation 2:5 when He addresses the church in Ephesus. Though they were active and disciplined, they had forsaken their first love. They had neglected their relationship with Him. As a warning—and an invitation—Jesus tells them to remember where they had fallen from, to repent, and to *do the things they did at first*. The same truth applies to marriage.

When we abandon our relationship with our spouse—whether through neglect, distraction, or unresolved hurt—the path to restoration begins by returning to what once mattered. To rekindle the flame, we must go back and do the things we did at first.

What initially drew you to one another? What conversations, gestures, and acts of care once made love grow? Where did the pursuit go?

Somewhere along the way, many couples stop doing these things. Life becomes busy. Responsibilities multiply. Disappointments pile up. And slowly, without realizing it, the first love is forgotten—not because it disappeared, but because it was no longer nurtured.

As the Lord changed my heart, He taught me how to love again—not conditionally, but selflessly. Love was no longer about what I received, but about how I served. God showed me how to put my wife before myself, how to listen, how to care, and how to return to the small but meaningful actions that once communicated love.

This genuine transformation is what drew her heart back toward me. It wasn't pressure. It wasn't persuasion. It was authenticity. She saw a love that was real—rooted in Christ—and it awakened a desire in her to experience that same love. Ultimately, it was the love of Christ that renewed our hearts and restored our marriage. As God healed us individually, He healed us together. What once seemed lifeless was revived. What seemed impossible became testimony.

Rekindling the flame is not about recreating the past—it is about allowing God to create something new. When Christ becomes the source of your love, even the coldest embers can be brought back to life. Nothing is beyond His reach. No marriage is too far gone. And no flame is too faint for Him to rekindle.

A Crown of Glory

Throughout Scripture, a crown is never merely ornamental. It is a public declaration of honor, authority, and responsibility. The Bible speaks of crowns as symbols of glory, righteousness, faithfulness, and reward. To wear a crown is to be *recognized*—not only for who one is, but for how one lives. Isaiah describes God's people as "a crown of glory in the hand of the Lord," emphasizing that glory is something *seen*, displayed, and held with care. Likewise, Proverbs teaches that an excellent wife is her husband's crown. In biblical thought, a crown does not elevate the wearer for pride's sake; it reveals the fruit of character, stewardship, and covenant.

A king without a crown may still possess strength, wisdom, or lineage, but to the watching world he appears as any other man. The crown announces his position. It tells a story before he ever speaks. In the same way, God designed marriage to tell a story.

Metaphorically, a wife functions as a crown to her husband. Not because she exists to decorate him, but because her presence, character, and conduct *reveal* the kind of man he is. How she speaks, how she loves, how she carries herself, and how she interacts with others on his behalf all silently proclaim something about the man who walks beside her. She announces—without words—whether he is a man of honor, humility, and godliness.

This imagery does not diminish the woman; rather, it elevates her role. A crown is never hidden. It is placed in the highest position, visible to all. To be called a crown is to be acknowledged as a sign of dignity and value. Just as a king is accountable for how he wears his crown, a husband is accountable for how he nurtures, honors, and protects his wife. Protection brings us to another biblical image: covering.

Scripture often uses the language of covering to describe God's care for His people. God is portrayed as a refuge, a shield, and a shelter—One who covers His children from storms they cannot withstand on their own. In marriage, this divine pattern is reflected, not replaced.

Just as an umbrella shields a person from harsh elements—rain, wind, and burning sun—so a husband is called to be a covering for his wife. This covering is not control; it is responsibility. It speaks of protection, provision, intercession, and presence. A covering does not dominate what it covers; it absorbs the impact so the one beneath it can stand secure.

The apostle Paul speaks of order and covering in relationships, ultimately pointing back to God Himself as the source of all covering. God is the covering of man, and man, under God's authority, is to be a covering for the woman. This establishes not superiority, but accountability. A man cannot rightly cover a woman unless he himself is first covered by God.

When these images come together, marriage is revealed as both glory and shelter. The woman, as a crown, reflects honor and dignity. The man, as a covering, reflects strength and protection. Both are dependent on God, who alone is the ultimate source of glory and refuge.

In a healthy, God-centered marriage, the crown is honored, the covering is trusted, and God is visibly present. The world may not understand the language of covenant, but it recognizes the evidence of it. Just as a crown announces a king, a godly marriage announces the reign of God in the lives of those who wear it.

Your Testimony is a Weapon

Just as a crown announces to the world that the man wearing it is a king, so a godly marriage announces to the world that there is a God who cares deeply about humanity. It proclaims that God is not distant or indifferent, but loving, intentional, and actively involved in the lives of His people. A healthy, restored marriage becomes a visible declaration of God's heart—a living witness that He still heals, restores, and redeems.

God has always chosen to reveal Himself through people. He displays His love, patience, mercy, and power not only through Scripture, but through transformed lives. Marriage, when surrendered to Him, becomes one of the clearest stages upon which His glory is displayed. It is not perfection that testifies of God, but transformation.

Scripture makes this truth unmistakably clear. Revelation 12:11 tells us that the saints overcame the enemy by two things: **the blood of the Lamb** and **the word of their testimony**. The blood of Jesus is the foundation—it secures victory. But the testimony is the proclamation of that victory. It is the evidence that what Christ accomplished on the cross is still effective today.

A testimony is a powerful weapon when used in the right context. It silences accusations, dismantles lies, and confronts despair. It declares to the world that the power found in Christ is not theoretical, but real. A testimony says, *"This is who I was, this is where I was headed, and this is what God has done."*

When applied to marriage, a testimony becomes even more profound. A transformed marriage announces that what was once broken can be healed, what was once dead can live again, and what once seemed impossible is not impossible in

Him. It confronts the cultural narrative that relationships are disposable and love is temporary. Instead, it declares that covenant still matters and redemption is still available.

Your testimony of a changed life—and a changed marriage—gives others hope. Hope is often born not from sermons, but from stories. When people see a marriage that has moved from chaos to peace, from bitterness to forgiveness, from distance to intimacy, they begin to believe that healing might be possible for them as well.

There is power in what is seen. An unspoken sermon often preaches louder than one shouted through a bullhorn. A marriage that has been genuinely healed by God does not need constant explanation or public announcement. Its fruit speaks for itself. The way spouses speak to one another, honor one another, and walk together through difficulty quietly proclaims a message that words alone cannot carry.

People will notice the transformation. They will sense that something is different. They may not have the language to explain it, but they will recognize the peace, the unity, and the strength that stands in contrast to what they have known. And eventually, they will ask how it happened.

At that moment, your testimony becomes a weapon— not against people, but against the enemy's lies. It declares that

God is faithful, that His Word is true, and that His love still changes lives. A restored marriage does more than bless the couple within it; it becomes a beacon of light, pointing others toward the God who makes all things new.

Christ & His Bride

From the opening pages of Scripture to its final chapter, God tells one continuous love story—a story of pursuit, covenant, sacrifice, and restoration. Marriage is not a side illustration in this story; it is one of its central metaphors. God chose marriage as the earthly reflection of a heavenly reality: Christ and His Bride, the Church.

The apostle Paul makes this unmistakably clear when he speaks of marriage and then declares, "This is a great mystery, but I speak concerning Christ and the church." In other words, human marriage was never meant to exist merely for companionship, social stability, or personal fulfillment. It was designed to point beyond itself—to reveal the heart of God and the redemptive love of Christ.

Christ is the Bridegroom. The Church is His Bride. And the way He loves her becomes the blueprint for how love is meant to look within marriage.

Christ does not abandon His Bride when she is

unfaithful. He does not withdraw when she is weak. He does not shame her when she is broken. Instead, Scripture shows us a Savior who pursues, cleanses, restores, and lays down His life for the one He loves. He covers her, sanctifies her, and calls her glorious—not because she earned it, but because He redeemed her.

This is the love story written throughout the Bible. From Genesis, where God seeks fallen humanity, to the Gospels where Christ gives Himself for sinners, to Revelation where the Bride is presented radiant and restored, Scripture consistently reveals a God who refuses to give up on His covenant people. Redemption is not an interruption to the story—it *is* the story.

This is why marriage matters so deeply to God. A husband is called to love his wife as Christ loves the Church—not selectively, not conditionally, but sacrificially. A wife is called to respond in trust and partnership, just as the Church responds to Christ. Together, marriage becomes a living picture of grace: imperfect people held together by a perfect God.

When a marriage is broken, it does not mean the picture is lost forever. It means the picture is incomplete.

Broken marriages are not evidence of God's absence;

they are opportunities for His redemption. The same power that raised Christ from the dead is able to resurrect what feels lifeless in a relationship. What feels too far gone to repair is not beyond the reach of the Redeemer.

Throughout Scripture, God specializes in restoring what others would abandon. He restores broken covenants. He heals hardened hearts. He brings beauty from ashes and life from graves. And He does not exclude marriage from that promise.

If you are holding this book with a weary heart—if trust has been fractured, communication eroded, or hope diminished—know this: your marriage is not disqualified from God's redemptive story. The same Christ who remains faithful to His Bride stands ready to heal, rebuild, and renew your union as well.

Restoration begins not with perfection, but with surrender. It begins when both hearts—wounded or willing—agree to trust that God can do for them what they cannot do for themselves. Just as salvation is not achieved by human effort, marital redemption is not sustained by human strength alone. It is sustained by grace.

God's true purpose for marriage has always been one of hope, love, and reflection. Hope, because no story is ever finished with God. Love, because covenant love reflects His own heart. Reflection, because marriage was designed to mirror the relationship between Christ and His people.

When a marriage is healed, it does more than restore two individuals—it testifies of a faithful God. It declares that redemption is real, covenant still matters, and love rooted in Christ endures. This is the crown. This is the testimony. This is the covering.

Marriage, redeemed by God, becomes a living gospel—one that points beyond itself to the ultimate Bridegroom who never fails, never leaves, and never stops loving His Bride.

And in that truth, there is always hope.

Chapter Seven Reflection

Marriage was never meant to be sustained by human strength alone. From the beginning, it was designed to be upheld by divine love—love that redeems, restores, and remains faithful even when hearts grow weary. As you reflect on this chapter, consider how deeply God has woven His own love story into the covenant of marriage.

Throughout Scripture, God reveals Himself as a faithful Bridegroom who refuses to abandon His Bride. Again and again, He pursues what is broken, redeems what is lost, and restores what appears beyond repair. This is not just a theological truth—it is a personal invitation. The same God who redeemed Gomer, Ruth, Israel, and the Church is still redeeming marriages today.

Perhaps as you read, you recognized places where love has grown cold, where forgiveness has been withheld, or where hope feels fragile. Maybe you saw yourself in the wandering bride, or in the weary spouse who has grown tired of pursuing. The beauty of the Gospel is this: Christ meets us exactly where we are, not where we wish we were.

Marriage reflects Christ and His Bride not because it is flawless, but because it is redeemable. The story God tells through marriage is not one of perfection, but of perseverance. It is a testimony that covenant love—when surrendered to Him—can outlast betrayal, disappointment, distance, and pain.

As you pause and reflect, remember this truth: your marriage is not defined by its worst season, but by the God who stands ready to redeem it. What feels incomplete is not finished. What feels broken is not beyond hope. God is still writing your story.

Chapter Seven Prayer

Father God,

We come before You humbled by Your love—the kind of love that never gives up, never turns away, and never fails. Thank You for revealing Your heart through Christ, our faithful Bridegroom, who laid down His life for His Bride.

Lord, You see every marriage represented here. You see the joy and the wounds, the faithfulness and the failures, the hope and the heartbreak. Nothing is hidden from You. We bring our marriages to You just as they are—unfinished, imperfect, and in need of Your grace.

Forgive us for the ways we have withheld love, chosen pride over humility, or allowed bitterness to take root. Teach us to forgive as we have been forgiven. Heal the places that feel beyond repair. Restore what has been lost through neglect, pain, or broken trust.

Jesus, be the center of our marriages. Rekindle what has grown cold. Strengthen what feels weak. Teach us to love not as the world loves, but as You love—sacrificially, faithfully, and without condition.

We surrender our expectations, our timelines, and our fears to You. We trust that You are able to do exceedingly more than we could ask or imagine. Let our marriages reflect Your

heart, Your faithfulness, and Your redeeming love.
We place our covenant in Your hands, believing that You are
still the God who makes all things new.
In Jesus' name, Amen.

Practical Takeaway

- *Return to the Source* - Before focusing on fixing your marriage, focus on deepening your relationship with God. Spend intentional time in prayer and Scripture, asking Him to shape your heart before addressing your spouse's shortcomings. Vertical restoration always precedes horizontal healing.

- *Practice Daily Grace* - Choose one intentional act of grace each day—an encouraging word, a kind gesture, a patient response. Grace does not ignore issues, but it creates an atmosphere where healing can grow.

- *Revisit Your "First Love"* - Reflect individually or together on the early days of your relationship. What actions, conversations, or habits once nurtured love and connection? Begin reintroducing those practices, not out of obligation, but out of intentional pursuit.

- *Speak Life, Not Accusation* - Commit to speaking words

that build rather than tear down. Replace criticism with honesty seasoned with love. Healing conversations require humility, listening, and a willingness to understand before being understood.

- *Let Your Marriage Tell the Story* - Remember that your marriage is a testimony in progress. You do not need to be perfect to reflect Christ—only surrendered. Allow God to use your journey, including the hard seasons, as a witness of His faithfulness.

- *Seek Support When Needed* - Restoration is not meant to be walked alone. Seek wise, godly counsel through pastoral guidance, Christian counseling, or trusted mentors. Asking for help is not a sign of failure—it is a step toward healing.

Closing Reflection

As this chapter—and this book—comes to a close, let this truth remain: Marriage is God's idea, sustained by God's love, and redeemed by God's grace.

No matter where you find yourself today, the ultimate love story is still being written—and God has not finished with you yet.

About the Author

David Mendoza III is a dedicated servant leader with a rich tapestry of experience spanning faith, service, and storytelling. Holding a seminary degree in biblical studies, he brings a deep understanding of faith and Scripture to his work. A retired federal law enforcement officer with over thirty years of service, David has dedicated his life to protecting and serving others. His military background as a Marine Corps veteran further underscores his commitment to duty and resilience.

David's passion for helping others extends beyond his professional life. He has served as a law enforcement chaplain, a peer support member, and a Veterans Support Program volunteer, offering guidance and support to those in need. Currently, David is a Christian minister and former pastor, sharing his faith and wisdom through his ministry.

He is the author of several award-winning books, including *Unleashed Redemption, Jed's Journal,* and a variety of captivating children's titles such as *Dakota – The Joyful Pony, The Biblical Adventures of Floppy and Hoppy, Gideon the Brave Bulldog, Wheezy & Goliath, A Lemon-flavored Popsicle, K9 Rudie: The Service Dog, Hero Bunny,* and *Don't Hang Around Turkeys,* all of which bring biblical narratives to life for the entire family.

David's life is a testament to the power of faith, service, and storytelling. He is a devoted husband of over thirty years, a father of two boys, and an active member of his church community, where he and his wife are deeply involved in adult and children's ministry. David's unwavering commitment to helping others, sharing his testimony, and offering support during times of need makes him a true inspiration.

David is reachable via email at *authordavidmendozaiii@yahoo.com,* or you can visit his website at *www.booksforhisglory.com* to get in touch.

www.ingramcontent.com/pod-product-compliance
Lightning Source LLC
Chambersburg PA
CBHW021104130626
46554CB00002B/529